Craft of
Whiskey Distilling

Published by the American Distilling Institute (ADI)

*The American Distilling Institute is the collective voice of a new generation of artisan distillers.
We are dedicated to disseminating essential information regarding the art and science of distilling.*

ISBN 978-0-9824055-1-2

For permission to reproduce any part of this book
please correspond directly with

White Mule Press
Box 577
Hayward, CA 94543

Visit the American Distilling Institute website at
www.distilling.com

Contents

STRANAHANS
COLORADO WHISKEY

2405

OFFICE

PRIVATE PARKING
WYATTS TOWING CO.
UNAUTHORIZED VEHICLES
WILL BE TOWED AWAY AT
VEHICLE OWNERS EXPENSE
303-777-2448

STRANAHAN'S
COLORADO WHISKEY

STRANAHAN'S
COLORADO WHISKEY

STRANAHAN'S
COLORADO WHISKEY

STRANAHAN'S
COLORADO WHISKEY

Preface

The new generation of artisan whiskey distillers, whenever possible, use local ingredients to reflect the region of the country where they are located. They also look to nearby microbrewers as a source of inspiration and sometimes wash. Brewing and distilling go hand in hand because the mash-tun can produce wort for brewing or wash for distilling.

To distill whiskey you first have to make beer. Beer is a technical term for whiskey wash, regardless of the type of raw ingredients used. The microbrewer uses a mash-tun to produce a sweet barley water called wort. The same mash-tun can also be used to make wash for whiskey distillation. The difference is that distillers wash is un-hopped, contains no solids and most importantly, it will ferment in less then a week.

The new generation of craft whiskey distillers, like Scottish distillers, will use a mash-ton to produce all malt whiskies. They will use numerous beer recipes to produce a new generation of barley, rye and wheat whiskies. These whiskies will have flavor and character not found in commercial corn whiskies. I also think that we'll soon see a new generation of whiskies infused with wood (apple, cedar, birch) and spices.

Craft distillers don't need a column still with two dozens of plates to make whiskey. Visit any small whiskey distillery and you will see that most have a still without column and plates. And, if they do have a column still, it will be used to make stripping runs with plates open. Then they make heads and tails cuts on the second spirits run using one plate. Every distillery works differently. The key is to make head tail cuts that save congeners (flavors) that define the style of whiskey you are distilling.

Special thanks to Ian Smiley, who wrote the heart of the book, Distillation Principles. Also thanks to contributing writers Alan Dikty, George Ferris, Eric Watson, Zac Triement, Bill Smith, and Attorney Robin J. Bowen. Artwork is by Catherine Ryan and layout is by Uri Korn. To learn more about craft distilling, join the American Distilling Institute (ADI) at distilling.com. Member support helps educate the public about craft distilling.

Bill Owens, President
American Distilling Institute

The purpose of this manual—
a barrel a week

Introduction

This manual is intended for the craft whiskey distiller who aims to make excellent-quality malt whiskey through artisan distillation methods. This manual describes, at the craft level, the process of making whiskey. It gives detailed instructions on how to distill one barrel (53 gallons) of 120-proof malt whiskey.

The reader learns about the principles of distillation, types of stills, and the process of distillation. The manual also goes into detail about how-to make head and tails cuts—the elusive operation that a distiller needs to learn in order to create a world class whiskey.

Most important is the chapter on mashing and creating a barley wash for fermentation. The all-grain recipes in the manual are adapted from the mashing (brewing) process used by commercial malt whiskey distilleries. Finally, the wash will be distilled using the double-distillation method employed by most of the renowned malt-whiskey producers.

The quantities in this manual are stated in Standard American Weights and Measures, and temperatures are in degrees Fahrenheit.

DEFINITION OF "CRAFT" OR "ARTISAN" DISTILLER

Craft distillers produce alcoholic beverage spirits by distillation, or by infusion through distillation or re-distillation. Maximum production for a "craft" or "artisan" distiller should not exceed 250,000 proof gallons per year. The "craft" or "artisan" distiller utilizes a pot still, with or without rectification columns, for distillation of beverage spirits. A distiller starting with neutral spirits produced by others, who redistills without substantially altering the neutral character of the spirit may not be said to be a "craft" or "artisan" distiller.

Glossary

abv Alcohol by Volume.

Aldehyde A volatile impurity found in heads; often redistilled separating it from alcohol.

Barrel (Wooden) 53 U.S. gallons, 44 Imperial gallons or 200.6 liters.

Barrel (Beer) 31 gallons.

Beer Stripping The process of running wash through a still (no head or tail cuts) to remove alcohol that will be redistilled. A stripping run usually starts at 170 proof and ends at 70 proof .

Beer Stripper A large pot still, without plates, used to strip wash for a second distillation.

Bubble Caps Caps sit on trays over vapor tubers in the column still (spirits still). Caps provide contact between the rising vapors and descending reflux crating a distillation cycle and enriching the alcohol.

CFR Code Federal Regulations; U.S. Government regulations, "Type of Definition" for example: rye whiskey must be fermented mash of not less that 51% rye and stored in a new oak container.

Charge The volume of wash to be distilled.

Condensor The apparatus, often a tube in shell, in which a vapor condenses to liquids.

Congeners Impurities. This minor chemical gives liquor (spirits) a distinctive character and flavors. It's found in both heads and tails,

Dephlegmator A chilling apparatus (condenser) at the top of the reflux column. It is comprised of a bank of tubes with cold water running through them. This increases reflux, and the purity of the distillate.

Dextrose Basic sugar know as corn sugar. A base for distilling whiskey (moonshine).

DSP Distilled Spirits Plants; a federally licensed distillery.

Double Distilling A process where the distillate is distilled twice. The first time to remove alcohol and the second distillation is make cutting the head and tail cuts.

Fractional Distillation Done in column still using plates and bubble caps. The process separates spirits into different volatility.

Heads Is the first spirits off the still, contain several undesirable chemical such as aldehydes. Heads are collected and then often re-distilled as distillers try remove the flavorful congeners.

Mash Is produced by mixing hot water and grains.

Mash-Lauder A process that mechanically mixes barley and water.

Mash Tun A double jacketed tank in which hot water and grains are mixed. The tank (mash-tun) has a false bottom (a screen or slotted tubes) allowing the sweet barley water to drain. Distiller collects the barley water for fermentation. After fermentation it becomes wash that is then distilled.

Moors Cap A still with a flat top (hat). The cap catches reflux, sending it back to the ketle for re-distillation.

NGS Neutral Grain Spirits. (190+ Alcohol). In the USA it is produced from corn. NGS is used by distilleries around the world for blending, vodka, gin, whiskey, etc. It is the workhorse of the distillation industry and used by many distilleries producing hundreds of products.

pH A measure of the acidity or alkalinity of a solution, equal to 7 for neutral solutions—increasing with alkalinity and decreasing with acidity. The pH scale ranges from 0 to 14.

Parrot A device that looks like a parrot, the bird, with a long beak. It holds the hydrometer—collects and cools alcohol running from the still. This allows the distiller to know the percent of alcohol flowing from the still.

Proof An American term used to determine the strength of the alcohol: for example, 120 proof is 60% alcohol or abv.

Reflux When vapors in the still are cooled they fall back into the still as liquid. The amount of the reflux obtained depends on the shape of the still and the angle of the lyne arm.

Reflux Column A column which cycles liquids through two or more distillations. Used to make NGS.

Spirit Still A still designed to do the final distillaiton producing finished whiskey.

Spirit Run The final distillation that produces the finished whiskey.

TTB Tobacco Tax and Trade Bureau formally BATF. It licenses and collects taxes from U.S. distilleries.

Tails Alcoholic distillate containing a high percentage of fusel oil.

Tote A large stainless steel tank for transporting and storing spirits.

Wash Fermented barley water.

1

Distillation Principles

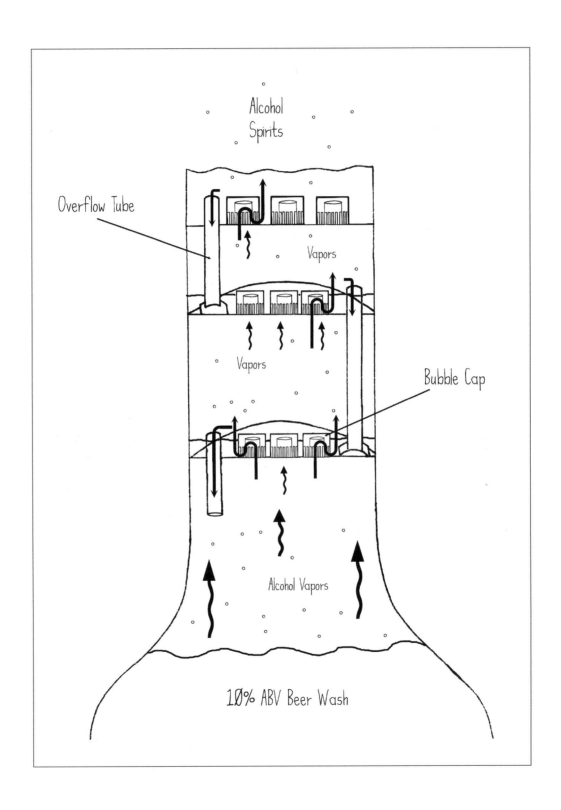

Most artisan stills are of the reflux or pot column design because of the inherent flexibility that they offer.

HOW DISTILLATION WORKS

Distillation is a physical process where compounds are separated by virtue of their different boiling points and vapor pressures.

The separation in distillation occurs when a mixture of compounds in the still is brought to boil. As a simplification, assume that the still contains only ethanol and water. Ignoring the azeotrope discussed below, for every mix ratio of ethanol to water there is one and only one new boiling point that lies between the boiling point of either. Conversely, for each boiling point, there is one and only one ratio of ethanol in the kettle, and an enriched ratio in the vapor and the distillate. If you know the temperature in the kettle, you can look up the exact ethanol ratio both in the kettle and in the vapor/distillate, in a simple table [figure 1/page 5].

Assume a mixture of 90% water and 10% ethanol (by volume) is to be separated by distillation. Water has a boiling point of 212°F and ethanol has a boiling point of 173°F, but this 10% ethanol mixture will boil at 197°F; it will not boil at 173°F. The vapor above the liquid will be 61% ethanol, as will the distillate. In a simple kettle, the ethanol percentage will drop during the boil because more ethanol than water is being removed, and neither are being replenished. This alone accounts for the increase in boiling point from start to finish— the ratio changes, so the BP changes.

Note that we started with 10% ethanol in the kettle, and now have a distillate at 61% ethanol, a 6-fold increase in strength. Referring to the table and graph below, if we now distill this condensate again, the new distillate will be 86%, and if we distill that, we will have a 91%, and again 92%, and again 93% and after six distillations, we may get 94%. As the concentration of the impurity (water) decreases, it becomes more difficult to remove. This notion is very important for other products of fermentation in our wash. No matter what the concentration and boiling point of a given impurity, some of it will escape the kettle and find its way to the distillate throughout the distilling run. This means that head cuts can never be precise because these lighter impurities do not all vaporize before the hearts begin. Likewise, some tail impurities manage to vaporize well before they are expected. Compounds with boiling points between water and ethanol, such as diacetyl at 190°F may be impossible to remove by distillation. Therefore, distilling a bad wash never makes a good whiskey— and a good whiskey always starts with a good wash.

High-separation vodka stills employ a reflux column with many plates where vapors can condense, then like small kettles, re-vaporize the new enriched liquid, further enriching the vapor. Multiple cycles of condensation and re-boiling, one cycle per plate, occur in a single pass as vapors rise through the column before distillate is drawn from the still near the top. Even these stills can not enrich beyond 96.5% ABV because ethanol and water form an azeotrope where some mix ratios have a boiling point not between the boiling points of the constituents. This prevents complete distillation. Nonetheless, reflux columns attached to pot still can sharpen separation, making head and tail cuts easier, but most believe that this leads to a lesser whiskey because the cleaner separation strips away character. Artisan distillers want to preserve the character of their whiskey, so if a column is employed, the plates are opened to reduce reflux and more closely match the results from the neck and arm of a traditional whiskey still.

If your kettle temperature is 198.5°F then your kettle contains 9% ethanol and the vapor contains 59% ethanol. As the run goes on, ethanol is removed from the kettle, the kettle temperature rises toward 212°F and the vapor concentration decreases.

THE DIFFERENT TYPES OF STILLS

There are a number of different designs of stills. The most basic design is a "pot still," with a pipe leading from the lid into a condenser coil. The condenser coil can either be long enough to air cool the vapors or it can be shorter and immersed in a water jacket. Such a still affords minimum separation since there is almost no separation of the vapors once they leave the boiler. Although this design of still is not suitable for producing beverage alcohol by modern standards, it will still concentrate an 8 or 10% abv wash to 60% in a fairly fast run.

The next type of still is the "whiskey still," sometimes called a "gooseneck still." This design is technically a form of pot still and has been in use for centuries for commercial whiskey production, and is just as popular today in modern whiskey distilleries as it has ever been. A whiskey still has a large boiler with a long broad neck rising from it. The neck bends at the top and leads to a condenser coil immersed in water. This design is very similar to the crude pot still, except the tall broad neck affords enough separation to hold back most of the fusel alcohols from the distillate while retaining the desired flavors in the finished spirit. They are suited to the production of whiskey, brandy, rum, schnapps, and other non-neutral spirits, for which they are very widely used commercially. However, the whiskey still is not suitable for the production of vodka, gin, or other spirits derived from neutral alcohol, which requires a high-separation still capable of producing pure ethanol.

This brings us to the high-separation still design called a "column still" or a "fractionating still." A fractionating still is used to produce pure ethanol by fractional distillation for vodka and gin, or for pharmaceutical and laboratory use.

[Figure 1] This is a table and graph of boiling points for ethanol/water mixtures by volume. (Hint— copy this and paste it onto your still).

BP (F)	kettle%	cond%
212.0	0	0
210.0	0.87	12
209.3	1.25	18
207.5	2.5	28
205.7	3.75	36
203.9	5	43
202.1	6.25	50
200.3	7.5	54
198.5	9	59
197.6	10	61
195.8	11	65
194.9	12	67
190.4	19	75
186.8	25	79
182.3	36	83
178.2	58	86
177.1	67	87
176.4	72	88
175.6	76	89
174.2	84	90
173.8	85	91
173.1	89	92
172.8	94	95
172.6	96.5	96.5

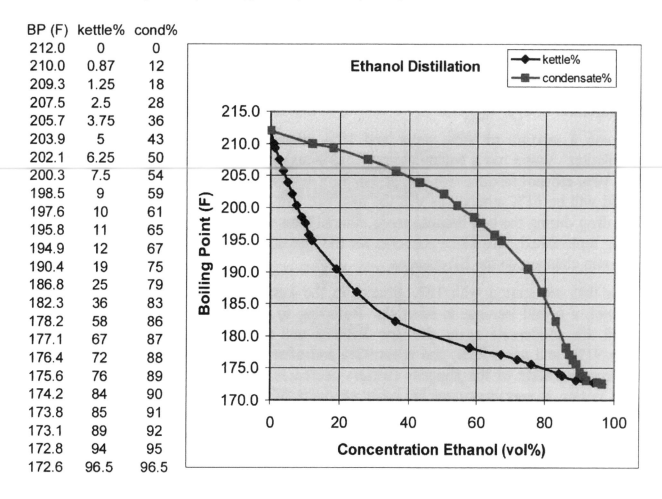

In smaller fractionating stills the vapors emerging from the boiling mixture pass up a column packed with small pieces of glass, ceramic, stainless steel, copper or other material, inert to the process. This material is called the "column packing." In larger fractionating stills, the columns have baffle plates with holes or bubble caps instead of packing material. Each piece of packing, or bubble cap, can hold a small amount of liquid, either internally (if they have internal crevices) or in the interstices between adjacent particles. At the top of the column, the emerging vapor is condensed into a liquid by means of a heat exchanger with cold water running through it. The condensed liquid runs back down the column until it reaches the boiler where it is reheated, converted into vapor once more, and once again moves up the column.

At equilibrium, which takes about an hour to achieve in the case of pure-ethanol production, the system consists of vapor rising up the column meeting a flow of liquid running down the column from the heat exchanger. At each vapor-liquid interface on the packing material within the column, a partial separation occurs wherein the more volatile components of the mixture go into the vapor phase and rise while the less volatile components go into the liquid phase and are carried down toward the boiler. At equilibrium, the various components in the mixture become stacked up in the column in the order of their boiling points, the most volatile at the top and the least volatile at the bottom.

There's a variation of fractionating still called the "continuous-run still." With the continuous-run design of fractionating still, the fermented wash is fed into a small boiling chamber from a reservoir and is vaporized immediately upon entry to the chamber. The different components of the mixture are drawn off at various heights along the column, and the spent residue is drained off at the bottom. This process can continue indefinitely as long as fermented wash is fed into the boiling chamber. Acetone, for example, would be continuously drawn off from the top of the column while ethanol would be continuously drawn off from a point a little further down.

The last still design to be discussed in this text is the "reflux still." A reflux still is very similar in design to the fractionating still except it doesn't have a heat exchanger at the top of the column forcing a complete condensation of all the vapor that reaches the top. It has a packed column like a fractionating still, but the vapor that reaches the top exits to the condenser and is received as output. While a reflux still benefits by the purifying process of the redistilling at the packing surfaces like a fractionating still does, without the forced reflux of a top heat exchanger it doesn't produce as pure a neutral ethanol as a fractionating still. However, reflux stills are very commonly used in the artisan distillation of whiskey, and other non-neutral spirits, and it's this type of still that will be discussed in the rest of this text.

Most artisan stills are of the reflux or pot column design because of the inherent flexibility that they offer. The best known manufacturers of pot and reflux stills are: Vendome, Holstein, Christian Carl, and Forsyth. The Index contains a complete list of manufactur-

ers. These brands of still come with multiple bubble-cap trays, and each tray can be bypassed by operating a lever. These stills can also be purchased with a dephlegmator, which is a chilling apparatus at the top of the column comprised of a bank of tubes with cold water running through them to increase the reflux, and therefore the purity of the distillate. The still can be operated with the dephlegmator disabled, or with cold water running through it at whatever rate the operator chooses. Between the variability of the dephlegmator and the ability to bypass, or not, the multiple bubble-cap trays, just about any level of separation can be achieved with these artisan stills. That's why they make such excellent whiskey stills.

THE FLAVOR OF SHAPE

The whiskey still has four parts: pot, swan neck, lyne arm, and condenser. The shape of each section affects rectification and the taste of the spirits. Ther eated (to 172°). It can be heated by direct fire, steam, gas, or wood. All systems have advantages and disadvantages. There is no right way to heat wash. Most manufacturers, however, prefer a double-jacketed steam-water system that provides a gentle heat to the wash. Mainly, you don't want to burn the wash. Most pots have a sight glass so the distiller can check for foaming during the distillation process.

■ The swan neck sits on top of the pot. It can be tall, short, straight, or tapered. Often the swan neck is connected to the pot via an ogee, a bubble-shaped chamber. The ogee allows the distillate to expand, condense, and fall back into the pot during distillation. Most pot stills have a tapered swan neck, allowing for better separation and better enriching of the spirits during distilling.

■ The lyne arm sits on top of the swan neck. It can be tilted up or down, and it can be tapered or straight. Most arms are tapered down. Often pot stills are fitted with a dephlegmator, or what the Scots call a purifier. The dephlegmator is fitted with baffles that use water plates or tubes to cool the distillate, sending 90 percent of it back to the pot. Its main purpose is the enrichment of the spirits before they're sent on to the condenser.

■ The condenser, or worm is used for cooling the spirits and providing a small stream to a collection tank or pail.

DISTILLATION PROCESS

In distilling parlance, the compounds in the wash that are not ethanol or water are called congeners. Some congeners such as acetaldehyde, methanol, and certain esters and aldehydes, have boiling points lower than ethanol, while certain other esters, the higher alcohols (fusel alcohols), and water, have higher boiling points than ethanol. This means the lower-boiling-point congeners come out in high concentration at the beginning of the distillation run, and the higher-boiling-point ones come out in high concentration towards the end of the run, leaving the ethanol as the most abundant compound during the middle of the run.

So, when distillation takes place in an artisan still, such as the reflux stills discussed above, the distillate that comes out is divided into three phases called: heads, hearts and, tails. The heads contain the unwanted lower-boiling-point congeners that come out at the beginning of the run, and the tails contain the unwanted higher-boiling-point congeners that come out at the end of the run. And, the hearts are the desired spirit.

Since whiskey is not distilled at a high-separation level, it means that each phase bleeds into the adjacent phase. That is to say, there's a considerable amount of ethanol in the heads phase, and there are late heads congeners at the beginning of the hearts phase. Similarly, there's a significant amount of early tails congeners at the end of the hearts, and there 's a considerable amount of ethanol in the tails phase. The hearts are the whiskey, and while they are comprised mostly of ethanol and water, they have a delicate balance of late-heads and early-tails congeners that make up the flavor profile of the whiskey.

Since both the heads and the tails contain a lot of ethanol and residual desirable flavor, they are mixed together and saved for future recovery. The heads and tails when mixed together are called feints. They can be distilled separately to produce another whiskey run, or they can be mixed in with a future spirit run, where their ethanol and flavors are recovered as a part of that run. However, each subsequent distillation produces its own set of heads, hearts, and tails, and the feints from those runs are also saved for future recovery.

When whiskey is made, it's usually done in two distillation runs: a beer-stripping run; and, a spirit run. The beer-stripping run is generally done in a larger, high-volume pot still called a beer stripper. The beer stripper is used to distill the fermented mash and concentrate the ethanol and all the impurities into a distillate of about 35% ethanol, called low-wine. The spirit-run is done in a smaller whiskey still, either a gooseneck or an artisan reflux still, called a "spirit still." The spirit still is used to distill the low-wine and refine them into the finished spirit. There are the two outputs retained from the spirit-run: the finished spirit; and, the feints

For a beer-stripping run, the fermented mash, which is typically about 8% abv, is loaded into the beer-stripper, and the contents are brought to boil. Since this run is just a primary distillation, the heads, hearts, and tails are not separated out. The entire output from this run is collected in a single lot, and the run is continued until the aggregate percent alcohol is down to 35% abv. This distillate is the low-wine, which is the input to the spirit run.

To produce the finished whiskey, the spirit still is filled with the low-wine from the beer-stripping run, and often a measure of feints from previous spirit-runs. The spirit still is then brought to boil. It is with the spirit run that the distiller adjusts the boil-up rate to achieve a gentle, slow flow of distillate and carefully separates out the heads, hearts, and tails.

Some whiskey distilleries produce their whiskey in one single distillation. In effect, they do a spirit run directly from the wash. The artisan reflux stills discussed above are excellently suited to doing this type of whiskey distillation, but operationally it's very labor in-

POT STILL CONSTRUCTION

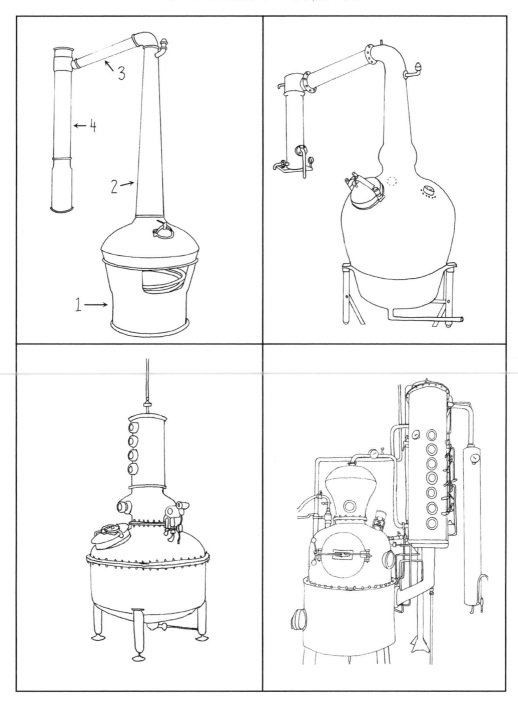

tensive and a lot of attention must be paid by the distiller to numerous smaller runs rather than one larger run.

Some people find the whiskey from a single distillation run to be richer and to have a more natural flavor, while others find it to be harsh and unrefined. In this text, the more-common double-distillation method is used.

MAKING THE CUTS

Probably the most elusive part of the distilling process for making whiskey, is making the cuts from heads to hearts and then to tails. Making a cut from one phase to the next is the point where the distiller switches the output so that itís collected in a different receiver than the previous phase. At the end of the spirit run, the heads will be in one container, the hearts in another, and the tails in a third one. The question is, when to switch from one phase to the next?

Experienced distillers do this by taste. Even though there are measurable parameters like still-head temperature and percent alcohol of the evolving spirit that can be used to judge when to make the cuts, taste and smell still remain the most reliable method of determining them.

The empirical parameters for judging the cuts are: the percent alcohol of the spirit that's flowing out of the still (i.e. the evolving spirit); and, the still-head temperature. However, these vary from one still to the next, and vary based on the properties of the low-wine (e.g., percent alcohol, and quantity). It is possible to develop a consistent process using the same still and the same quantity and a formulation of low-wine, such that the parameters remain the same for each run. For example, if a spirit run is being done in an artisan reflux still with low-wine that is 35% abv, the begin-cut (i.e. the cut from heads to hearts) is usually done when the evolving distillate is at about 80% and when the still-head temperature is about 180 degrees. And, the end-cut (i.e., the cut from hearts to tails) is often done at about 65% and when the still-head temperature is about 200 degrees. However, a spirit distilled from a straight malt wash, can often be end-cut as low as 60%. It's because of these nuances that smell and taste become the only truly reliable indicators of when to make the cuts.

When making the begin-cut, the taste characteristics that the distiller is looking for are as follows. When a spirit run comes to boil and the first d istillate starts flowing from the still, this is the beginning of the heads phase. The distiller can collect a small sample of the distillate on a spoon or in a wine glass and smell it. At this stage, the distillate will have the sickening smell of solvents like nail polish remover or paintbrush cleaner. However, before long this solvent smell will diminish, and even when a sample is tasted these compounds will be very faint. As the solvent character disappears completely, the distillate will start to take on a hint of whiskey flavor. This flavor will increase until it becomes very pronounced and highly concentrated. It's when this flavor is clearly evident (i.e., more than just a hint) but is still increasing in intensity that the distiller cuts to the hearts phase.

To make the end-cut the distiller needs to monitor the flavor of the hearts through the following changes in taste. At the beginning of the hearts phase, the intensity of the whiskey flavor will still be increasing, and will continue to do so until it becomes very strong. However, as the hearts continue, the intense whiskey flavor will fade into a smooth, sweet, pleasant flavor that will persist for most of the hearts. The flavor will change slightly as the hearts progress but it will remain sweet and pleasant. Towards the end of the hearts, the flavor will start losing its sweetness and a trace of harsh bitterness will being to appear in the flavour. This harsh, bitter flavor is the onset of the tails. While a small amount of this bitterness is considered to contribute to the "bite" character of the whiskey, the distiller should cut to the tails receiver before mush of it is allowed to enter the hearts.

The tails can be collected until the evolving distillate is down to about 10% and the still-head temperature is about 210 degrees. The reason for doing this is to render all the residual alcohol that's left in the still at the end of the hearts phase. This alcohol can then be recovered in a future spirit run.

The tails phase starts out bitter, and the bitterness becomes more intense as the tails continue, but as the tails progress, the bitterness subsides and gives way to a sweet-tasting water. This sweet water is called "backins."

2

Malt Mash for Whiskey Production 250 Gallons for Stipping

… there are two schools of thought in the artisan segment regarding how a whiskey wash should be distilled.

With the "new" artisan distilling movement in the US, the availability of hand crafted super premium spirits has resulted in an impressive array of locally and regionally produced spirits for consumers. Although there are artisan spirit producers that have been around for close to 30 years now, the rapidly growing interest in entering this exciting industry segment started to occur about 5 years ago.

In the last couple of years the interest has swung towards producing darker spirits, particularly whisky, which conveniently is mirroring consumer trends. So far, unfortunately, most of those entering this industry do not have a brewing background. Due to the lack of experience and/or training in the art and science of brewing, there is a void that must be filled to be successful in making a whisky that meets and hopefully exceeds consumer expectations.

This chapter is intended to introduce the concepts of mashing malted barley for the production of single malt whisky without becoming too technical, but rather to introduce the fundamentals required to successfully produce a wash that once distilled can become a great dram.

Before getting into the details, it is necessary to define some basic terms. All of these terms are defined as they relate to the production of single malt whisky using professionally designed and built equipment:

Combi-Tun A single vessels that combines both the functions of a mash tun and a lauter tun. Although a cheaper option and a space saver, the use of a single vessel for both functions can limit your production capacity since you cannot lauter and mash at the same time.

Doughing In Term for mixing water and malt together when preparing a mash.

Foundation Water This is the water that is initially introduced into the mash tun to both warm it up and to fill the combi-tun with water to a level 1 to 2 inches above the lauter screen. This fill level prevents the malt from clogging the mash screen while you are doughing in.

Grist The ingredients used to make a mash.

Grist Hydrator A device used to spray hot water into the crushed malt as it enters the mash tun which aides in proper hydration which is required for effective and efficient starch conversion.

Hot Liquor Tank A fancy name for a giant water heater. This tank is used to heat the dough in water that you will introduce slowly into your grist and later to raise the temperature of the water to sparge with.

Lauter To separate the liquid "wort" from the malts after mashing has been completed.

Lauter Tun Term for a vessel where a completed mash is transferred to allow for the separation of the malt grains ("draff") from the liquid portion which is known as "wort" (pronounced "wert") or in distilling terms, "wash." The name of this vessel comes from the German word lautern which means "to filter."

Lauter Screen Also known as a false bottom, this wedge wire screen rests above the bottom of the lauter tun to allow the wort to run off while leaving the grains behind.

Malted Barley The seed of the barley plant, which is a type of grass, that has been soaked in water and allowed to germinate just until the sprout is visible at the top of the seed and small rootlets develop. The germinated barley is then kilned to stop the germination process. This kilning keeps the embryonic plant from consuming too much of the starch as it's energy source for growth. It is this starch that we wish to harness for conversion into fermentable sugar which is made possible through the development of enzymes during the malting process. In addition to making starch accessible, the kilning process also develops the malt flavor we associate with whiskey.

Mash The mixture of malted barley and water prior to fermentation.

Mashing The process whereby hot water is mixed with malted barley and held at a temperature which will allow the enzymes created during the malting process to convert the starches in the malt to sugars that are fermentable, which in this case is mostly maltose, hence the origin of the word "malt.-"

Mash Tun Term for a vessel where the malted barley and hot water are mixed and held at a certain temperature to allow for the conversion of the starches to fermentable sugars.

Mash Tun Thermal Mass This is a fancy term for heat that is lost through a mash tun. If you pre-heat the mash tun with hot water to above the temperature of that which you intend to mash prior to doughing in, the thermal mass is 0. In the interest of simplicity, I am using the assumption that you are following this common practice. If you are not, then some more elaborate calculations are required to determine this loss because every mash tun varies in it's ability to hold heat. To determine thermal mass of a cold vessel requires empirical data specific to the subject vessel from which you can then derive the factor to use in calculations. This topic is beyond the scope of this chapter.

Sparge To introduce hot water beyond that of the water used to complete the mashing process with the purpose of rinsing as much sugar as possible from the mash. The use of this technique reduces the size of the vessel required to complete the mashing process which is a cost and space saver.

Tincture of Iodine Used to test for the presence of starch in a mash runoff. Place filtered runoff on a white plate in a thin layer, put a small drop of iodine in the layer. If the color changes little, there is no starch left in solution. If the color changes to blue or black, you need to rest the mash further.

Wash This term denotes a fermented solution which may or may not include solids that is placed in the still for distillation.

Before continuing into the technical details of mashing it must be noted that there are two schools of thought in the artisan segment regarding how a whiskey wash should be distilled. There are some that believe a greater character can be derived by charging the still with the whole wash without separating the grains from it. One positive attribute of this is that if fermentation is undertaken on the whole mash, the resultant wash will yield slightly more alcohol due to continuing conversion during fermentation. The negative impact of this practice is that by not separating the wort from the grains, your still charge will be significantly reduced versus just filling it with the wort. It is interesting to also note that all Scotch distilleries lauter their wort. This is not mandated by law like many of their practices so it is either a historical practice or they feel that there are benefits to separating the grain from the wort. So, this is a subjective choice rather than a objective technical mandate.

Lautering the Wort

The below details are based upon lautering the wort. If you intend to not lauter, ignore the lautering instructions, but all of the other concepts still apply.

GRIST COMPOSITION

Single malt whisky can be made from a blend of many types of malted barley but most are made from a single type. That being stated, I am of the belief that blending malt types such as 2 row pale, Munich, aromatic and biscuit for example, is an under explored topic that could offer a substantial level of differentiation. Presently there are a few artisan distilleries that are sourcing their wort from a brewer's regular wort stream (not custom made for the distillery) that is part of their usual beer production and can serve as an illustration of this concept.

For the greatest depth of flavor, ease of starch conversion and the highest yield, it is best to use a 2 row pale ale malt that is fully modified. This is the malt most commonly used by craftbrewers and is readily available. If a phenolic note is desired in the finished whisky, that effect can be realized by blending in either peat smoked malt (Hugh Baird from the UK is a leading supplier to distilleries) or for a more subtle effect, rauchmalt from Germany may be used. You could also smoke your own malt with wood blends that could become a signature note to your whisky! This is done to produce the much lauded Smoked Porter, a beer produced by Alaskan Brewing Co. They smoke their own alder wood at a salmon smokery near the brewery.

Before mashing the malts must be crushed. To properly crush malt requires a mill that is specifically designed for crushing malt. The use of other types of mills will grind the grain and pulverize the husks. Maintaining husk integrity is crucial because it helps to clarify the lauter runoff and keeps the lauter screen from plugging up. A proper grist has little flour and could be described as somewhat "grit like" with mostly intact husks.

WATER

There are many topics that can be discussed when addressing water used in mashing. Rather than go into detail regarding water chemistry, I am going to assume that the water you plan to use is low in iron, contains no sulfur and meets potability standards for drinking water. If you are going to be using municipal water, you will need to pre-filter the water to remove any chlorine, chloramines or other chemicals that are either volatile or could compromise fermentation. It is best to have an independent lab test your water rather than using an average water analysis from the local water department. They can test for dimensions that are important for brewing that water departments have no need to test for.

It is crucial for proper starch conversion to make sure the pH of your water is below 7. The optimal pH of a mash is 5.2. You can adjust the mash directly, but it is safer to adjust the dough in water in case you undershoot the pH which could compromise the mash.

To start, adjust the pH of the dough in water to 6 and then see what the pH of the mash is once doughed in. The two best agents to adjust pH are food grade phosphoric or lactic acid and are inexpensive. For those who do not want to use these naturally derived acids, you can use sauermalz which is an acidified malt made in Germany which brewers there use because they are not allowed to use acids to lower pH.

Another method to adjust pH would be to make a small "soured mash" by using lactic acid producing bacteria to ferment it. This technique is in essence how the aforementioned sauermalz is made. Attempting to use this technique would require a lot of experimentation and may take a while to reach the desired result consistently. Another concern if this method is employed is that you run the risk of contaminating the pure yeast cultures used in regular fermentation or/and cross contamination of your plant.

You could also use the "set back" which is the wash that is left in your still after a run. The concentration process of distillation also concentrates the acidic nature of wash. But, this concentration can vary from time to time so developing a consistent dosing into a mash might prove difficult.

To test pH of mashes, paper test strips should not be used because of lack of range and the darkness of the mash makes readability difficult. It is best to get a lab grade pH meter from a scientific supply vendor. Make sure to get one that is automatically temperature compensated (ATC) and has a replaceable probe that is high temperature rated and will work properly in protein containing solutions. Do not use a pH meter designed for gardening. A pH meter requires calibration before each use. Purchase a meter that calibrates using two buffer solutions, one that is pH 4 and the other, pH 7.

MASHING

The following example involves using a combi-tun which is the most common mash/lautering system. In some plants, a mash mixer and a lauter tun are used. This type of system increases plant efficiency because while the first mash is being lautered, you can begin making another mash. In this style of system, the mash mixer is usually directly heated via low pressure steam. The downside is the additional expense of having two separate vessels and the additional space that is required.

The below example also utilizes a hot liquor tank for the preparation and introduction of water for both the dough in and sparging steps. This is preferred so that you can mix the water with the malt directly into the combi-tun. A grist hydrator is also used so that you can slowly mix the water with the malt to produce a uniformly hydrated and smooth mash. It is possible to dough in without one, but starch balling is inevitable if you simply dump

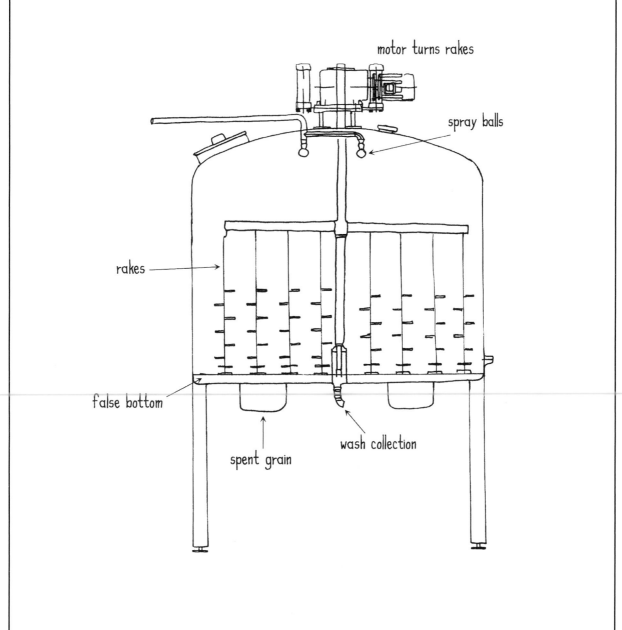

motor turns rakes

spray balls

rakes

false bottom

wash collection

spent grain

Mash-Lauder Tun: A double jacked tank equipped with a raking arm that mixes barley and water together producing a sweet barley water that distillers call wash. The tun has a slotted metal false bottom allowing the wash to be separated (drain away) from the grains. It is then sent on to fermentation. The mash-tun rakes now push the grain out of the ton and sent for disposal (pig or cattle farm). Finally, spray balls are used to clean the tun.

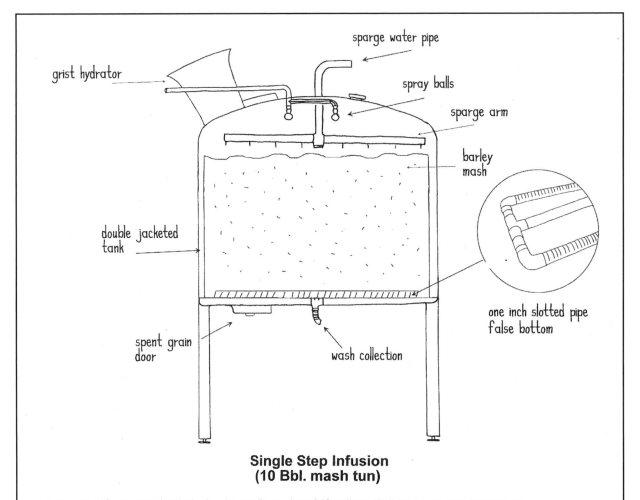

**Single Step Infusion
(10 Bbl. mash tun)**

A mash-tun without a mechanical rake can easily produce 250 gallons (8 bbls.) beer wash for distillation.

1. Start by laying down a three inch foundation (165 degree water) on top of the false bottom in the mash-tun. Now using the grist hydrator, mash-in 650 lbs, 2 row barley. The final "rest" temperature of the mash should be 152 degrees. (A mash as low as 140 or as high 160 degrees will also produce wash for fermentation)

2. Barley enzymes created by mixing hot water and malt together will covert starch water to sugar water in 30 minutes. This process creates the wash for distillation. Now, start slowly draining (collecting) the wash from the tun and sending it to the fermentation tank. While doing this turn on the sparge water and start "rinsing" the grain bed with185 degrees water. This process is also called "slip and slide". You slip out the wash while sliding water on the top the bed. A slip and slide balance is needed to keep the grain bed from collapsing slowing down and sometimes stopping the flow.

3. Use a 10 bbl fermentation tank to collect 8 bbls. (250 gallons) of wash. Cool the wash to 72 degrees and pitch the yeast. The 3 bbl tank head space provides ample head space for fermentation.

4. The original gravity (OG) of the wash before fermentation should be 1.070. After fermentation the final gravity (FG) of the wash should be 10.10 yielding 8 % ABW. (alcohol by weight) for distillation. Finally, drain remaining liquid from the mash-tun allow the grain and cool. One hour later dig out the mash and use the spray balls to clean the tank.

the crushed malt into the hot water. Visually it can appear that you have broken up all of the starch balls with a mash paddle, but in truth there will still be small clumps that encapsulate the starch which reduces extraction efficiency. A grist hydrator is easy to purchase or build and is worth the effort and expense.

The formulation of the grist is based upon targeting an ABV of 8%. The example uses a 8 barrel brewing system which will yield 250 gallons of lautered wash. The extract yield was calculated at a 75% mash efficiency which is the average for professionally built and operated combi-tuns. It is possible that before maximizing your mashing practices that the efficiency may be lower and therefore you may not collect 8 bbl. of wash at 1.074 SG (17.87 Plato, 18.7 Brix). If that is the case, you can use more malt to make up for the difference. ALWAYS REMEMBER: It is the starting gravity of the wash that determines when to stop filling a fermenter, not the total volume. The experience and empirical data gained through subsequent batches will allow you to maximize the yield at the proper gravity.

So, let's get mashing!

PREPARE THE HOT LIQUOR

• The grist to water ratio for this example is 1.3 quarts of water to 1 pound of grist. (1.23 l water to .45 kg. grist). I have chosen this ratio to ensure that both the malt and the hot liquor can fit in the combi-tun. Since beer brewing equipment is made with the knowledge that the mash will be sparged, this ratio is close to the maximum of what a combi-tun can accommodate. A thicker mash would serve as a buffer for enzymatic activity and therefore limit starch to sugar conversion which in the case of producing a distiller's mash would be counterproductive.

In making washes for distilling we are more concerned with a maximum amount of yield per pound of grist since we are not targeting the contribution of un-fermentable components that are important for flavor and body in the wort as is the case in brewing beer. If you are fortunate enough to be able to use a thinner ratio you will still have to keep in mind that you will need to make sure that you still will use enough water to sparge the mash properly otherwise you will leave extract behind.

• If your water chemistry requires it, filter through carbon media and/or treatment equipment recommended, installed and maintained by a professional water treatment company.

• Adjust the pH of the water to 6.

• Set the temperature controller to heat the water to dough in temperature. This temperature needs to be set so that once your mash is doughed in you will be at the proper temperature for conversion as combi-tuns are rarely directly heated. To determine the proper temperature you need to take into account heat losses through piping and pumps as well as determine how much temperature is lost due to the starting temperature of the malt comprising the grist. These losses will vary from plant to plant. In this example I have used 12 deg. F which is the loss I experience at my facility.

Below are the inputs used to calculate the requirements of the mash:

Grist Temperature — 75 degrees F. (24 C)

Ingredients 690# — 2 Row Great Western Malt (Canada)

Targeted Mash Temperature — 155 deg. F (62.8 C)

Dough In Water Volume — 227.7 gallons
(861.9 l, 7.34 US bbl.)

Mash Tun Thermal Mass — 0 (assumes no heat loss to the mash tun)

Heat Loss Due to Piping/Pumping — 12 deg. F (-11.11 C)

Heat Loss to Grist — .017 deg. F per pound of grist at 75 deg. F. (-17.76 C
per .45 kg grist)

Water Volume Lost to Grist — 690 # Grist X .12 Water Loss per #
= 82.8 gallons (313.4 l)

Therefore...

Grist Heat Loss — .017 X 690 pounds grist @ 75 deg. F = 11.7 deg. F
(-11.27 C)

Piping Plumbing Heat Loss — = 12.0 deg. F (-11.10 C)

Total Heat Loss — = 23.7 deg. F (-4.61 C)

Targeted Mash Temperature — = 145.0 deg. F (62.80 C)

+ Total Heat Loss = 23.7 deg. F (-5.4 C)

Dough In Hot Liquor Temperature — = 168.7 deg. F (75.94 C)

So, for this example, you would set the hot liquor temperature to dough in at 169 deg. F (76.1 C)

Sparge Water — Beyond the 228 gallons that needs to go into the mash, you will also need to know how much sparge water you will need to make up for the water that was absorbed by the grain (82.8 gallons) and that to reach a fermentable volume of 250 gallons.

Therefore...

Dough In Water Volume — 227.7 gallons (861.9 l, 7.34 US bbl.)

• Water Loss to Grain 82.8 gallons (313.4 l) = Mash Tun Wort
Volume: 144.9 gallons (548.49 l, 4.67 US bbl.)

Fermentable Volume Targeted: 250.0 gallons

• Mash Tun Wort Volume: 144.9 gallons = Makeup Sparge
Water Required: 105.1 gallons (397.83 l, 3.39 US bbl.)

Now, I wish this calculation was that easy, but it is not. This does not take into account how much foundation water you put in the mash tun prior to doughing in. It also does not take into account how much loss to deadspace that is present in your vessel nor the piping leading to the hydrator and sparge mechanism. These variables are different for every system and must be accounted for to achieve consistent results. The biggest thing that this calculation does not account for is the water that remains after you have stopped sparging. To sparge properly you must maintain the 1.5 to 2" of sparge water above the top of the grain bed to ensure that all of the mash is rinsed equally. Since the geometry of mash tuns can vary, the amount of additional sparge water you will need to prepare will also vary from system to system. The first time you produce a mash, make sure to have more water prepared than you will need. Take detailed water usage notes from that session and then you will know the right volumes of water for subsequent batches.

The above calculations can be done for you using inexpensive software that also helps with formulation and fermentation tracking. The best one is ProMash which has a very robust set of tools that is well suited to mashing and fermentation for a distillery. ($24.95, www.promash.com).

PREPARE THE COMBI-TUN

• Introduce the foundation water through the grist hydrator. This pre-heats the mash tun. Stop the fill when the water level is 1 to 2" above the mash screen.

• Begin introducing the hot liquor and grain simultaneously through the grist hydrator. Control the introduction of both water and malt so that while constantly stirring the two with a mash paddle, you can produce a smooth mash with no lumps. For a seven barrel mash, this should take at least 30 minutes.

• Once dough in is complete, put the mash tun cover back on to help retain heat. Take a temperature and pH reading to see how close you came to the target of 145 deg. F (62.8 C) and pH 5.2. If you did not nail these targets, make a note of how far you were off so you can determine what adjustments are required for subsequent batches.

• Re-set the hot liquor tank's temperature controller to 190 deg. F (195 deg. F — my 12 deg. F temperature loss would result in a 183 deg. F sparge water temperature. This is to prepare the water for sparging. If you have a recirculation loop (hopefully!) serving the hot liquor tank, make sure it is operating to prevent temperature stratification. The reason for the high temperature is to reduce the viscosity (thickness) of the mash liquid so it runs off freely. Although viscosity reduction is desired in runoffs for beer production, this high of a temperature is not used because it would carry over tannins into the finished product rendering it harsh. Since we are distilling off the liquid, this is not a concern.

• After the mash has set for 45 minutes, take a small sample of the runoff, filter it through a coffee filter to remove any grain specks and test it for conversion using tincture of iodine. (see procedure in definitions section). If the test is negative, you can begin sparging, otherwise, you must continue mashing until you reach a negative result.

• After the mash has passed the iodine test, introduce the sparge water slowly and indirectly so that it does not channel the mash. Allow the water level to rise 1.5 to 2 inches above the mash bed before starting the runoff. Slowly allow the wort to runoff at the same rate as you are introducing the sparge water. Doing so any faster will run the risk of plugging up the mash screen or channelizing the mash which will leave extract behind. A lauter time of 60 to 90 minutes is normal.

How do you know when to stop running off?

Contrary to what you might think, it is not "when the fermenter is full." It is when the contents of the fermenter are at the target gravity. We are targeting an 8% ABV in our fermented wash.

The formulation above should yield a starting gravity of 1.074 SG (17.87 Plato/18.7 Brix) and if fermented properly will finish at 1.012 SG (3 Plato, 8.95 Brix). Reaching these targets will yield a wash with 8.16% ABV.

Note: Brix readings are typically taken using a refractometer due to accuracy and ease of use.

Once a solution begins fermenting the alcohol in solution changes how light is refracted. The Brix figures for finishing gravity above are corrected for this refractive difference. The aforementioned software, ProMash, has a built in calculator to accomplish this conversion.

As the wort is running off, take frequent measurements at the fermenter to make sure that you reach the target SG.

It is important to make sure that the wort is aerated with either sterile air or pure oxygen as it is being sent to the fermenter. Yeast require oxygen to prepare for their reproductive phase. After that point, the environment must be kept anaerobic. NEVER introduce oxygen after fermentation has started! Aeration is typically accomplished through an in-line air "stone" that is attached to the outlet of the heat exchanger. A stone can also be installed in the fermenter to achieve the same result. Simply bubbling oxygen or sterile air into the fermenter without a stone will not be very effective because the bubbles must be quite small to go into solution. If you use pure oxygen to aerate, it is very important to not use too much oxygen as it is toxic to the yeast and will lead to poor fermentation results. If you use an oil less compressor equipped with an air drier and a sterile air filter, it is not possible to over aerate the wort.

Make sure to only pitch yeast after the wort is 70 - 72 deg. F (21 - 22 C). During fermentation yeast produce a good bit of heat which can raise the temperature of the wort up to 12 degrees F or more. If the wort is cast into the fermenter at a higher temperature than that and the yeast is added, it can seriously affect the fermentation outcome and possibly kill enough yeast that it barely ferments. For whisky, make sure to set the temperature controls no higher than 80 deg. F to maintain a proper fermentation.

3

Distillation
Principles

WHISKEY DISTILLING PROCESS
Double Distilling

1 Mash-Lauter tun, 2,000 lbs of barley malt, producing 33 barrels of 9% wash. (Just under 1,000 gallons).

2 Fermentation tank should yield 950 gallons of wash. The F-2 secondary tanks, hold bight beer wash prior to distilling.

3 The 450 gallon wash still now makes two stripping runs. (No plates).

4 Collection tank now holds 290 gallons of 35% low wines or 70 proof spirits.

5 In the 90 gallon (340 liter) pot-column still. (Plates open). Make 3 spirit runs doing head and tails cuts. Final yield, 100 gallons of hearts at 60% avb. (120 proof). For barreling.

6 Barrel six months to two years, dilute whiskey to 40% abv. or 80 proof for bottling.

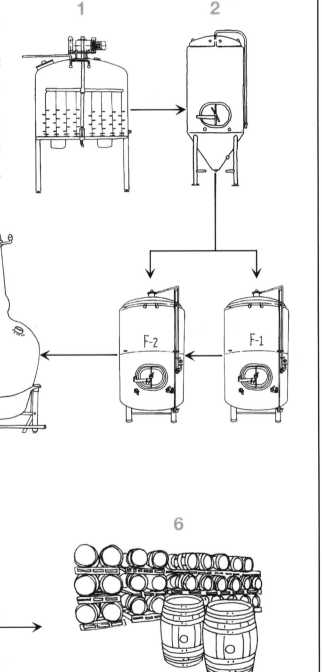

Whiskey in North America is distilled in two different ways. One is by continuous distillation in a column still, and the other is by an intermittent process in batch stills.

The aim of this chapter is to provide detailed instructions on how to distill the 945 gallons of malt wash produced in Chapter 3 to produce 53 gallons (1 barrel) of 120 proof (barrel strength) malt whiskey. The instructions are based using the 240-gallon copper pot still to do the primary distillation, and the 90-gallon German pot still to do the second (final) distillation.

BACKGROUND

Whiskey in North America is distilled in two different ways. One is by continuous distillation in a column still, and the other is by an intermittent process in batch stills. Batch stills are stills that have a pot that is filled with a fixed quantity of the substrate to be distilled (i.e. a batch). There are basically two methods of pot distillation.

Method One Two distillation runs are done using the same still for both runs. The spirit still is run with the plates open, and a primary distillation is done on all the wash. This run produces a low wine of 25 to 55% abv depending on the alcohol of the wash and speed of the run.

Then a spirit run is done on the low wine produced by the primary distillation using the same still with one plate down to produce a yield 70 to 75% abv. This is watered back to 60% abv and barreled.

Method Two The two distillations are done in separate special-purpose stills, namely a "wash still" and "spirit still". The wash is distilled in the wash still to produce a low wine of 25 to 55% abv. The low wine is then distilled in the spirit still to 70 or 75% abv. This is watered back to 60% abv for barreling.

BEER-STRIPPING

The first step in distilling whiskey is to do a crude primary distillation of the wash called a beer-stripping run. The output of a beer-stripping run is called low-wine, and the low-wine is the input to the final distillation (i.e., the spirit run), which produces the finished whiskey. The beer-stripping runs will be done in a larger still of 240-gallons capacity. Since there are 945 gallons of wash to be stripped and the capacity of this still is only 240 gallons, the wash will be stripped in four 235-gallon runs.

The purpose of the beer-stripping is to concentrate the alcohol and the congeners in the wash into a substrate of about 35% abv.

To do a beer-stripping run, the 240-gallon still is loaded with 235 gallons of wash, and the steam heat is applied to the boiler. When the wash comes to boil, the heat should be adjusted to deliver a fast flow rate into the receiver. For a stripping run, there 's no need to separate out heads, hearts, and tails. The idea is to simply do a fast, crude primary distillation on the wash.

Initially, the percent alcohol of the aggregate distillate in the receiver will be well over 80% abv, but as the run progresses, the percent alcohol will drop. The beer-stripping is to be continued until the percent alcohol of the aggregate distillate is down to 25% abv. At this point, the still-head temperature will be close to 212 degrees.

Note: The percent alcohol to be monitored here is the entire aggregate of distillate in the receiver, and not the percent alcohol of the evolving spirit as measured at the parrot.

When the distillate is down to 25% abv, the still can be shut down and the residue drained. Repeat this process on the remaining three quarters of the wash.

When the entire 945 gallons of wash has been stripped, you will have a total of about 300 gallons or more of 35% abv. low-wine, and you will be ready to proceed to the spirit-run step.

SPIRIT RUN

The spirit run is the final distillation that produces the finished whiskey. It's done in a spirit still, and must be performed carefully at the proper heat level and flow rate, with the correct bubble-cap trays selected, and with special attention being paid to the begin- and end-cuts to ensure a proper separation of heads, hearts, and tails. Since there are 300 or more gallons of low-wine and the capacity of the spirit still is only 90 gallons, the low-wine will be distilled in four 75-gallon runs.

Double Distilling with a Column Still

1 Mash- lauter 2,000 lbs of barley grain. Fermentation producing 33 barrels of 9% was. (Just under 1,000 gallons).

2 Strip the wash making ten, 90 gallon "fast" runs with the plates open. No heads or tail cuts. Total collection from runs, 120 gallons of 35% abv. (140 proof).

3 Two spirits run, making head and tail cuts. Yield 100 gallons of 70% abv. (140 proof).

4 Barrel age. To bottle, dilute whiskey to 40% abv.

5 Note, because the still is small it takes 12 runs (at least two days) to produce 100 gallons of whiskey. Solution to the problem is using a large still for stripping and small still for the spirits run.

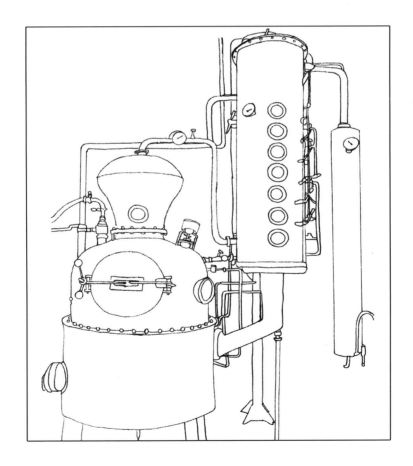

Single Pass Distilling with a Column Still

1 Mash- lauter 2,000 lbs of barley grain. Fermentation producing 33 barrels of 9% was. (Just under 1,000 gallons).

2 With to top plate close make 11 runs making head and tail cuts. Yielding 100 gallons of 65% abv. (140 proof).

Note: It would be very interesting to taste a whiskey that has been double distilled and a whiskey that was produced using single pass.

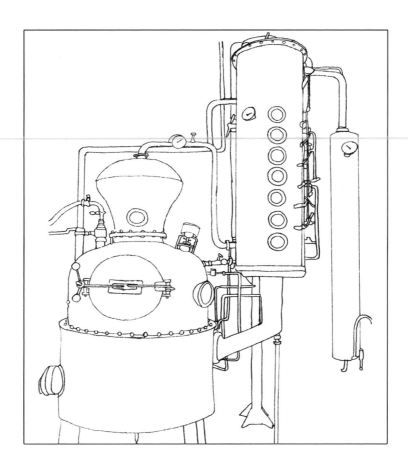

To do a spirit run, the 90-gallon spirit still is loaded with one quarter (approx, 75 gallons) of 25% abv low-wine, the required bubble-cap trays are enabled, steam heat is applied to the boiler, and the flow should be set to the heads receiver. When the wash comes to boil, the steam pressure should be adjusted to the correct level for running whiskey.

Initially, the percent alcohol of the distillate at the parot will be close to 90% abv and the spirit run will be in its heads phase. The distillate will be set to flow into the heads receiver at this point. As the run progresses, the percent alcohol at the parot will decrease. It's important that the distiller takes a small sample of the distillate every few minutes and smells and tastes it. At first, the distillate will smell of acetaldehyde and other pungent chemical-like smells. When such smells are evident, it's not necessary to taste the spirit. As the distillation continues, this chemical-like smell will diminish and the percent alcohol at the parot will decrease.

After a short while, the chemical-like smell will no longer be evident, and there will only be a faint taste of it. A little while longer, the distillate will smell and taste almost neutral. Shortly after this, the distillate will begin to taste of whiskey, and this flavor will become quite intense. This is the point where the distiller must begin-cut to the hearts phase, and set the flow into the hearts receiver. The percent alcohol at the parot at the begin-cut will be about 80% abv, and for a distiller not yet familiar with judging the begin-cut by taste, 80% abv at the parot is a good empirical measurement with which to judge the begin-cut.

As the distillation progresses, the intense whiskey flavor will subside and the distillate will take on a smooth, pleasant sweetness. This pleasant sweetness will continue but as the percent alcohol decreases, it will become more diluted tasting. And, as the tails phase approaches, a bitterness will begin to creep into the flavor, and past a certain point, although the distillate will still have a sweetness to it, it will no longer taste pleasant. It's around this point that the distiller should end-cut to the tails phase, and set the flow into the tails receiver. At the end-cut, the percent alcohol at the parot will be between 60 and 65% abv. An all-malt whiskey will usually end-cut a little lower than a corn or rye whiskey. It's quite common for a corn whiskey to end-cut at 64 or 65% abv, and for an all-malt whiskey to end-cut at 60 or 61% abv. Again, this empirical measurement is a good indicator by which a distiller can judge the end-cut if they are not yet familiar with judging by taste. At the end-cut, the distiller must set the flow into the tails receiver

The tails phase should be continued until the percent alcohol at the parrot is about 10%. The still-head temperature will be about 212 degrees, and the still can be shut down and the residue drained. At this point, the heads and the tails can be combined and stored as "feints" for future processing. Repeat this process on the remaining three quarters of the low-wine.

After the completion of the spirit runs, you will have close to 60 gallons of hearts at between 68 and 72% abv, and about 105 gallons of about 40% abv feints. Of course, these proportions can vary from one spirit still to another. Keep in mind, a subsequent batch made by this same formulation, would have the 105 gallons of feints added to the low-wine going into the spirit run, and would yield considerably more hearts than the 60 gallons from this very first run where there was no feints.

The 60 or so gallons of hearts are the finished malt whiskey and you will be ready to proceed to the barrel-aging step.

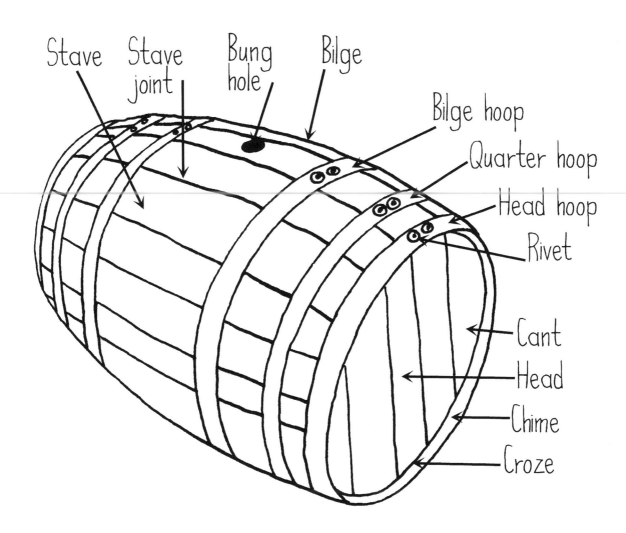

4

Barrel Aging

We do know that aging is related to the chemical changes that take place as a result of reactions with the alcohol and congeners in the spirit through oxidation and extraction of chemicals from the oak.

When new whiskey is freshly distilled, it's colorless and possesses only the flavor and aroma of the grain and the alcohol. It's from aging in charred oak barrels that the whiskey acquires its color, complexity, and richness of flavor. The aim of this chapter is to give an understanding of the barrel-aging process and its importance to the production of fine whiskey, and to provide detailed instructions on how to age the 53 gallons (one distillery barrel) of malt whiskey distilled in Chapter 4, and produce the final spirit.

BACKGROUND

It's still a mystery as to how the barrel confers its lubricious effect on the aging spirit. We do know that aging is related to the chemical changes that take place as a result of reactions with the alcohol and congeners in the spirit through oxidation and extraction of chemicals from the oak. Factors affecting this aging process are: percent alcohol of the spirit; the level of charring of the oak; the temperature and humidity in the aging warehouse; the size of the barrel; and of course, the length of time the aging takes place.

Percent Alcohol of the Spirit: The level of lignin fractions, lignin derivatives, vanillins, and tannin extracted from the oak, as well as the amount of congeners formed, are dependent on the alcohol concentration.

While a high-alcohol concentration, such as 80%, extracts more of the beneficial compounds and color, it can also extract more tannin, which imparts too much astringency and harshness to the flavor. Additionally, the higher the alcohol content, the more water that has to be added to dilute it to bottling strength when the aging is finished. This also dilutes the barrel contribution. So, it has been determined that for whiskey aging in new barrels, 55 to 65% abv is the optimum strength to achieve a balance of barrel extraction and color, with lower tannins. It also reduces the dilution of the barrel compounds at bottling time. However, this lower alcohol concentration also results in slower aging as the rate of chemical change and barrel extraction is reduced. Barrels that are used more than once can age stronger spirits since the harsh tannins have been diminished by the previous contents.

At 55 to 65% abv, barrels were found to have a greater porosity for water, with the fusel alcohols, acids, esters, aldehydes, and furfural being retained. Further studies confirmed that these lower strengths result in an increase in alcohol content after aging, whereas a decrease in strength is found when spirits are aged at higher alcohol concentrations.

Temperature and Humidity: The humidity in the warehouse also plays a significant role. High humidity usually results in a decrease in alcohol strength, and dry warehouses usually have the opposite effect. Humidity also affects the character of the final spirit. It has been found that the extraction of vanillin is better at low humidity. Low-humidity aging does generally result in spirits that have a better sensory quality.

The temperatures in the warehouse affect the oxidation reactions that take place in the spirit, and higher temperatures accelerate these reactions. Since these are great contributors to the aging of the spirit, it's obviously advantageous to age at higher temperatures. Acids and esters increase due partly to the oxidation of the ethanol to acetic acid via acetaldehyde which is then partially converted to ethyl acetate (an ester). Therefore, a consequence of aging is an increase in the concentration of acids, esters, furfural, tannins, and aromatic compounds as a result of oxidation, condensations, and other interactions with the wood.

Tropical temperatures, especially when there are variations between night and day, are ideal for faster aging, and it has been found that aging may not take place during the winter in temperate climates if the warehouse is not heated. Movement of barrels during the aging period will also help, but this is obviously not a practical approach.

TYPE OF OAK

The type of oak also plays a role. European oak is not as dense as American white oak, so you get a higher color but some harshness. It is also interesting to note that once-used bourbon staves shipped to Scotland are rebuilt with new, larger heads so that the 53-gallon barrels are rebuilt into 63-gallon hogsheads. The prior-contents of the barrel also influence the taste of the product to be aged. A sherry cask will give the spirit a more fruity character than a bourbon barrel, and if it was an Oloroso sherry, color development will be faster. New barrels will impart a darker color and richer flavor, but the more delicate spirits take on more harshness after aging.

THE LEVEL OF CHARRING AND THE USE OF OAK CHIPS (STAVES)

Spirits aged in charred barrels mature faster than those aged in toasted or non-charred barrels. The charring process for new barrels definitely contributes to the aging of a spirit. It acts like an activated-carbon filter to adsorb sulfur compounds and it provides a passage for the spirit into the pores of the oak. In the United States a full-depth charring of barrels (i.e., 1/8 inch) used to age American straight whiskey is predicated by law. This is in spite of the fact that over-charring can actually destroy some of the flavors that are needed to develop the finish of the spirit. This is why toasting, or even a light char, may be a better route, but it is illegal in the United States to age straight whiskies, such as bourbon, in anything but fully-charred barrels. A medium-depth char is required just to crack the wood, and a heavier char burns up wood compounds that would only be caramelized by a low- or medium-level char.

Charred barrels produce a deeper colored spirit (temperature is also a contributor) and there is a greater production of esters.

It has been found that the more delicate-flavored spirits like malt whiskey, Canadian whisky, and rum are overpowered by the oak contribution of new charred barrels, so these spirits are aged in once-used bourbon barrels, among other types of used barrels, to give a much more balanced flavor profile.

Toasted oak chips (or staves) can be added to a barrel to provide additional lignin and vanillin, this can augment the aging effect of a barrel. They do provide a significantly different congener profile than that produced by a once-used charred barrel. And, since putting toasted staves in whiskey barrels is legal in the United States, they are often used by bourbon distilleries to contribute an additional mellow sweetness to whiskey that would not normally benefit by this as much since the bourbon barrels are fully charred as per US law.

In summary, a charred barrel contributes color, vanillin, honey, spice, viscosity, and a myriad of other flavors to a whiskey that can be detected by the experienced taster.

ANGELS' SHARE

As spirits age in barrels, the porosity of the wood results in a certain amount of evaporation. In a standard distillery barrel (i.e. 53 gallons) about 10% of the remaining spirit in the barrels evaporates each year. And, it's not unusual for a barrel of fine 15-year-old single malt Scotch whisky to be less than half full when it's ready to be bottled.

This loss of spirit due to evaporation is affectionately known as "the angels' share.". Depending on the temperature and humidity conditions, discussed above, the evaporation will result in an increase in percent alcohol or a decrease. The actual increase or decrease is really a function of more water evaporating than alcohol, or vice versa. For example, high-humidity warehouses result in a decrease in percent alcohol, and lower-humidity ones result in an increase.

SIZE OF BARREL

All of the prior discussion on barrel aging and its associated properties has been based on aging spirits in a standard 53-gallon distillery barrel. For example, a top-quality bourbon is aged until it's "ready". Because bourbon, like all American straight whiskies, is aged in new charred oak barrels, there's a point in the aging process when the oak contribution can go too far, and the whiskey takes on a cloying, overpowering astringency. This is why bourbon distilleries monitor the taste of their aging whiskies frequently past a certain point to determine when it's "ready." And, this point tends to fall between six and eight years in the barrel. With bourbon, the saying "the older, the better" simply doesn't apply.

However, this six-to-eight-years applies to 53-gallon barrels. If a different sized barrel is used then the dynamics change, and values like length of time in the barrel, the rate at which lignin and vanillins are extracted, etc are completely different. The reason for this is volume increases by a power of 3 relative to the dimensions, while surface area only increases by a power of 2 relative to the dimensions. That is to say, the amount of surface area of wood per gallon of spirit is greater in a smaller barrel and less in a bigger barrel.

So, if a distiller aged his/her whiskey in 5-gallon barrels rather than 53-gallon ones, there would be a considerably greater surface area of wood exposed to a gallon of spirit than in a 53-gallon barrel. And, the whiskey ages much faster.

Smaller barrels age the whiskey faster and impart lignin and vanillin, and also tannin, faster as well. And, a good-quality bourbon can be aged out in only three to six months in a 5-gallon barrel. In fact, any longer and the whiskey would go over the top and become astringent and bitter.

It's important to note that the flavor profile is a little different for a whiskey aged in a smaller barrel, but not a difference that is necessarily inferior or superior. Also, the angels' share is greater for a smaller barrel, but this is amply mitigated by the dramatically shorter aging time.

Smaller barrels are much more expensive and take up more space in the warehouse than larger ones per unit capacity. For example, ten 5-gallon barrels would take up a lot more warehouse space than one 53-gallon barrel, and they would cost a lot more.

However, there's an increasing trend among small, start-up whiskey distilleries to use smaller barrels while they are getting established in the market place due to the fast turnaround on aging. The one aspect of starting up a new whiskey distillery that impedes most entrepreneurs is the long aging period of six to eight years before being able to start selling their product. Even the minimum of two years predicated by law is too long for most start-ups, and after only two years of aging, the product would be substandard and not likely to market well anyway.

However, with small barrels turning out an excellent product in only three to six months, starting up a whiskey distillery is feasible. And, after a distillery is well established, it makes sense to go to the standard 53-gallon barrel to realize the economies of scale.

AGING THE 53-GALLONS OF MALT WHISKEY PRODUCED IN CHAPTER 4

As mentioned above, American straight whiskies are aged in new charred oak barrels, while more delicate flavored spirits like the malt whiskey produced in the previous chapters are aged in used-once barrels, such as used bourbon barrels. So, to age our malt whiskey, an empty bourbon barrel is required.

PREPARING THE BARREL

If the barrel was recently emptied and there are no visible signs of major leakage anywhere on the barrel, then it's ready for filling. However, if the barrel has been empty for awhile, and the wood has dried out, the barrel will leak between its staves. So, it will have to be rehydrated to swell out the wood to close all the leaks. This is done by placing the barrel near a drain and filling it full of water with a hose. The barrel will leak so adjust the water flow so that the barrel stays full. It typically takes 24 to 48 hours for the barrel to seal itself, and the rate of filling can be turned down every few hours. If after rehydrating the barrel for 48 hours, there's still a leak between two staves, find where along the staves the water is leaking, and take about a 1/2 inch wood chisel and hammer it into the oak about a ° inch deep, and about a 1/2 inch from the seam between the staves. Do this on both staves on each side of the leak. Then take two small wedges of cedar and hammer one into each slit made with the chisel. This will tighten the seam between the two staves and seal the leak. Do this for all leaks between the staves. Once the barrel is sealed, it should be kept full of water until the whiskey is ready to go in.

DILUTING THE WHISKEY

As explained above, 55 to 65% abv is the optimum range of percent alcohol for barrel-aging whiskey, so for our malt whiskey we're going to dilute it to 60% abv.

In a vat capable of containing at least 53 gallons, prepare a 53-gallon quantity of 60% malt whiskey by diluting the hearts from the spirit run in Chapter 4 to 60% abv with pure water (i.e. distilled or RO water).

The dilution calculation should be done using the following formula:

Quantity of hearts = 53 X 0.6 / percent alcohol of hearts

Quantity of pure water = 53 - Quantity of hearts

Example: Say, the hearts were 70% abv

Quantity of hearts = 53 X 0.6 / 0.7 = 45.43 gallons of heart

Quantity of pure water = 53 - 45.43 gallons = 7.57 gallons of pure water

Of course, you may chose to dilute the entire quantity of hearts to 60% abv, and to do so, you would use the following formula to calculate the amount of pure water to add:

Quantity of pure water = Quantity of hearts X percent alcohol of hearts / 0.6 - Quantity of hearts

Example: Say, there was 60 gallons of hearts at 70% abv

Quantity of pure water = 60 gallons X 0.7 / 0.6 - 60 gallons = 10 gallons of pure water

On the other hand, you may not want to bother with calculations, so you could simply dilute the hearts to 60% abv by judiciously adding small amounts of pure water and mixing thoroughly until the alcoholmeter reads 60% abv.

Next, make sure all the water has been emptied out of the barrel and then fill the barrel with the 60% abv whiskey. Hammer a beech wood or poplar bung into the bung hole.

Then, place the barrel where it can be easily observed over the next couple of weeks. This is a period where the barrel is proofed to make certain it doesn't have any residual leaks. After the barrel is proofed and it's clear that the barrel is not going to leak, it should be placed in the location where it's going to be aged for a number of years.

As was pointed out above, hot places that experience temperature swings are the best locations to situate barrels with aging spirits, so the barrel should be situated bearing this in mind.

Also, if the barrel can be shaken or jostled back and forth periodically, this will speed up the aging process.

If the barrel is placed in a hot, reasonably dry location, and can be shaken occasionally, the whiskey will age out nicely in about three years. So, it's important that the whiskey be sampled every few weeks or every month after the first 18 months of aging.

To sample the whiskey, remove the bung and draw up about an ounce of it with a glass wine thief or a large pipette, and empty it into a wineglass. Take a nose and taste of the cask-strength whiskey, and then dilute it half-and-half with water and nose and taste it again. While the whiskey is still immature, it will have an unbalanced flavor of straight wood and a burnt taste. When the whiskey is "ready", it'll have a smooth, rich, balanced flavor with characteristics of the wood and char, but the raw woody, burnt taste will have subsided.

After determining that the whiskey is mature, monitor the development of the whiskey each week for several more weeks to make sure the whiskey has reached a mature, rich flavor, but where you sense that any more oak contact may take it over the top. It's best to have several people make these final evaluations.

At this point, the barrel should be emptied into glass or stainless-steel containers to halt the aging process. The container, or containers, should not have a lot of air space, and should be sealed up tight to prevent evaporation. The whiskey is now aged and ready for diluting, filtering, and bottling. The exact volume and percent alcohol of the whiskey should be measured and noted. You are now ready to proceed to the diluting, filtering, and bottling step. Both these methods involve double distilling, which gives smoother results, and is therefore what's recommended in this text.

5

Bottling

When whiskey in a barrel has reached its peak, it's impor-
tant that the whiskey be taken off the wood... If a whiskey is
aged too long in the barrel, it will become astringent and
bitter, and the flavor will lose its balance.

After the whiskey in the barrel has finished aging and is ready to be packaged, it must be prepared for bottling, and bottled.

The aim of this chapter is to explain the processes involved in the preparation of whiskey for bottling, and to give instructions on how to bottle the whiskey in the barrel from Chapter 5.

BACKGROUND

Throughout the barrel-aging process, the whiskey will have been tasted periodically so as to determine when it's ready for drinking. When the whiskey has a nice balance of caramels, lignins, vanillins, tannin bitterness, and the smell and taste of burnt wood has mellowed out into the rich and elegant flavor of good whiskey, it's time to take the whiskey off the oak, prepare it for bottling, and then bottle it.

When whiskey in a barrel has reached its peak, it's important that the whiskey be taken off the wood even if the facility is not ready to bottle it. If a whiskey is aged too long in the barrel, it will become astringent and bitter, and the flavor will lose its balance. So, when the whiskey is ready it must be moved out of the barrel and into containers made of inert materials such as glass or stainless steel. As long as the containers are tightly sealed so no evaporation can take place, the whiskey will keep indefinitely.

Volume and Percent Alcohol: The first thing that needs to be done when preparing the whiskey for bottling is to measure its exact volume and percent alcohol. The barrel will have started out with 53 gallons, but over the aging period, a certain amount of the whiskey will be lost due to evaporation, the angels' share.

The rate of evaporation is typically about 10% of the remainder per year. So, it would be quite normal for a barrel that's been aging for seven years to be down to 48% full

The formula for calculating angels' share is as follows

Final volume = Original volume X (1 ñ percent lost per year) number of years age

For 53 gallons aged for 7 years at 10% loss per year it would be

Final volume = 53 gallons X (1 - 0.1)^ = 53 gallons X 0.9^7 = 53 gallons X 0.47 = 25.3 gallons

However, if the whiskey is aged in a hot climate, the lost will be more like 15% per year, but it will age out in only 3 years. The angels' share under those conditions would be calculated as follows

Final volume = 53 gallons X (1 ñ 0.15)^3

= 53 gallons X 0.85^3

= 53 gallons X 0.614

= 32.5 gallons

Clearly, aging faster in a hotter climate reduces the loss due to angels' share.

Of course, the final volume must be measured empirically. The calculation is only used to determine if the empirical measurement is roughly where it should be. For example, if a barrel had a slow leak, more whiskey would be lost than would be by angels' share alone. The calculation would help to spot this inconsistency.

Also during this metamorphosis, the percent alcohol will change. It'll increase or decrease depending on the ambient temperature and humidity of the barrel warehouse, so the percent alcohol must be measured as well.

VATTING

"Vatting" is when a distiller blends various proportions of the same whiskey from different barrels to achieve consistency of quality and flavor. Different barrels will age the whiskey a little differently, and blending the whiskey from numerous barrels is a good way to maintain a uniform brand. Also, the whiskey will vary slightly from batch to batch, and vatting will even out those variations as well.

Vatting is not to be confused with the term "blending", where the distiller mixes various different types of whiskey, invariably from different distilleries, to achieve a unique flavor and brand of its own, different from any of the whiskies used in the blend. Also, such blends are often made using Grain Neutral Spirits (GNS) and other types of raw (i.e. un-aged) whiskies in the mix. Some whiskey blenders don't distill whiskey at all, and just buy whiskey from many dozens of distilleries that they blend together to make their own specific brands. Vatting is only the mixing of the same brand of whiskey from different batches and barrels within the same distillery.

If the distiller is going to vat his/her whiskey, the proportions from each barrel in the mix need to be worked out in small quantities by a panel of tasters. Once the proportions of each barrel of whiskey have been decided, the large quantities must be poured into a vat and mixed thoroughly. If the whiskey is not going to be vatted, then it can just be placed in the vat, ready for diluting.

Diluting: The whiskey straight out of the barrel will be between 55 and 65% abv, and it will require diluting to bottling strength. Whiskey is diluted to somewhere between 40 and 50% abv for bottling.

Before the distiller dilutes the whiskey right down to bottling strength, it must be decided whether the whiskey is going to be treated with activated carbon or not. Most whiskies are not treated with carbon, but if one is, it must only be diluted to 4% above the final bottling strength. It is further diluted after the treatment to the exact final percent alcohol. This is because the carbon treatment lowers the percent alcohol slightly, so there needs to be some leeway to take this into account.

If the whiskey is not going to be treated with activated carbon, but is going to be filtered, it should only be diluted to 2% above the final bottling strength. This is because the whiskey could pick up a small amount of water in the filtering process. Again, the final dilution to the exact bottling strength is done after. Diluting should be done with distilled or Reverse Osmosis (RO) water to avoid the water imparting any taste, and to prevent any mineral precipitation in the bottles.

Activated-Carbon Treatment: Most whiskies are not treated with activated carbon, but some are characterized as very mild, and a certain amount of this mildness is achieved by exposing the whiskey to activated wood charcoal. Incidentally, other types of activated carbon would strip too much flavor and aroma out. That's why wood charcoal is the type of carbon used. In some cases, the whiskey is poured through a deep bed of carbon, and in others the carbon is added to the vat, and it's gently agitated every few hours.

The optimum percent alcohol for carbon to work most efficiently is 38% abv. However, that's too low for any whiskey so the whiskey is diluted from its barrel strength to bring it closer to optimum, without going too low, before any activated-carbon treatment is done.

As mentioned above, the action of the carbon on the whiskey lowers the percent alcohol slightly so it's important that the whiskey not be diluted to its exact bottling strength before carbon treatment. Keeping it at 4% above the final bottling strength ensures it doesn't drop too low as a result of the carbon. After the carbon treatment and the filtering, the percent alcohol can then be adjusted to the exact final value

Filtering: Whiskey doesn't need much in the way of filtering. It's simply a matter of removing the wood and char particles picked up from the barrel during the years of aging. It's purely for aesthetic reasons, as having a bottle of whiskey that was slightly cloudy from suspended burnt oak particles would not be very appealing.

Most distilleries use a plate filter with coarse filter media to take out the particles. It's important to filter after diluting, and not before, to make sure any turbidity in the diluting water is removed as well. Also, the receiving tank for the filtered whiskey and all its tubing must be completely lint free, or particles could be re-introduced to the whiskey.

Bottling: The bottling of whiskey doesn't require the same level of sterilization as for bottling wine or beer. At 40 or more percent alcohol, whiskey is itself a disinfectant. However, it's very important that all the equipment and the bottles used are very clean.

A good type of bottling machine for spirits is an inline overflow filler. This type of filler is suited to filling containers where a specific visible fill level is required. The overflow mechanism enables the device to fill the bottles much faster since there's a provision to return overflowing liquid to the reservoir, thereby eliminating the need for a slow fill to achieve a specific level. Small inline overflow fillers are available at a very reasonable price that can fill several thousand bottles per day. Most craft distillers use a four head gravity filling machine or an enolmaster vacuum filling machine. These filling machines are readily available from wine equipment companies such as G.W. Kent (gwkents.com) or St. Pats (stpats.com).

Once the whiskey is diluted and filtered, it can be placed in the product tank of the bottling equipment, and bottled. It's interesting to note that once a spirit is diluted to bottling strength, it will actually improve with age for a few weeks. The reason for this is not fully understood, but recent research indicates that it takes a few weeks for all the different types of molecules to completely mix and diffuse themselves evenly throughout the substrate. And, this has a beneficial effect on mellowing and bringing out the complexity of the flavor.

BOTTLING PROCEDURE FOR THE BARREL OF WHISKEY FROM CHAPTER 4

This section describes how to bottle the fully-aged malt whiskey from Chapter 4. There should be about 30 gallons of cask-strength whiskey at about 60% abv.

Equipment

- 53-gallon barrel of malt whiskey from Chapter 4
- Distilled or RO water
- 50-gallon tote
- Measuring equipment (thermometer, alcoholmeter graduated cylinders)
- Plate filter with coarse-grade media
- Bottling machine and ancillary equipment

Method

First, the barrel is emptied into the vat and the exact quantity and percent alcohol of the whiskey is measured. Since there's only the one barrel, there won't be any vatting done.

Malt whiskey aged in a once-used barrel is not normally treated with activated carbon, so we won't be doing an activated-carbon treatment on the whiskey.

The target bottling strength is 43% abv, and since the whiskey is not going to be activated-carbon treated, but it is going to be filtered through a coarse plate filter, the initial dilution should be 2% above the final bottling strength (i.e. 45% abv). Knowing the exact volume and percent alcohol of the whiskey, dilute it to 45% abv using the following formula

Quantity of pure water = volume of whiskey X %abv of whiskey / 0.45 - volume of whiskey

Example: Say, there were 30 gallons of whiskey at 60% ab

Quantity of pure water = 30 gallons X 0.6 / 0.45 - 30 gallon = 10.0 gallons of pure water

After diluting the 30 gallons of 60% whiskey with 10.0 gallons of pure water, there would be 40 gallons of 45% whiskey. Next, the whiskey is filtered through a coarse plate filter to remove the tiny particles of wood and char. The plate filter should be set up with coarse filter pads that have been thoroughly wet with water. Before filtering the whiskey, run about 10 gallons of tap water through the filter to eliminate any cardboard-like flavor from the pads. Try and empty as much water as possible out of the filter unit after rinsing with the 10 gallons of water before running the whiskey through. It's important to make sure the receiving container is clean and lint free. After the whiskey is filtered, it can be diluted to its final bottling strength (i.e. 43% abv). To do this, it's best to run the diluting water through the filter after the whiskey to make sure it's completely particle free. This will also serve to rinse the last traces of whiskey left in the filter into the diluting water.

At this point, there should be more than 41 gallons of 43% whiskey ready to be bottled, Prepare the bottling machine and bottle the whiskey. This should produce well over 200 750ml bottles of malt whiskey. That's about 17 cases.

A

To-Do List
for starting a craft distillery

1

Get to know the other players in the market and become knowledgeable in the spirits market as a whole The American Distilling Institute is a good place to start (distilling.com).

2

Learn how to properly distill There are books and equipment manufacturer sponsored training courses as well as the American Distilling Institute hands on class.

3

Determine what types of sprits that you would like to manufacture and visit similar type distilleries.

4

Spend a significant amount of time on a business plan Statistics show that businesses that begin with a well thought out business plan have a significantly higher rate of success The process of writing the business plan will force you to dig deeper into the industry and the business When you are planning your financing, raise at least 25% more than you think you will need.

5

Determine your distillery's location, work with the local and state fire marshals, building inspectors and any local environmental agencies These groups can stop your business in its tracks; itís better to find out that a particular location will not work sooner than later

6

Order/purchase your distilling equipment. If you are buying new equipment, plan on 6-12 months from down payment to receipt

7

Begin developing your brand (s) keeping TTB guidelines in mind www.ttb.gov

8

Complete your Federal TTB and State liquor control commission licensing. Work on getting your bond first as that can take some time. Start with your insurance agency; they may work with a surety company.

9

Get to know the people in your state tourism office. This can be a good resource to build awareness about your new business

10

Develop a list of contacts at local newspapers and media outlets; use this group every time you send out a press release.

11

Determine the bottle/package that you plan to use. The glass market is tight at the moment; find a supplier and learn their ordering requirements.

12

Have a good attorney and accountant at the ready.

B

Formulas

So You Want to Be a Micro-Distiller?

Then you need to know about formulas.

Robin Bowman

You have your federal and state licenses— so what's next. Before you fire up your still, you should determine whether the distilled spirits product you intend to produce requires a formula approval by the Alcohol & Tobacco Tax & Trade Bureau (TTB). Federal law requires domestic distillers to submit formulas for certain distilled spirits products to TTB for approval before production can begin. Formula approvals are required in order to ensure that the products meet federal food safety requirements, are taxed appropriately, and bear labels that are not misleading to consumers.

To begin, not every distilled spirit requires a formula approval by TTB. TTB's formula regulations do not clearly identify which distilled spirits require formula approval. Rather, they state a general rule that requires distillers to obtain formula approval if they add

[1] In order to import certain foreign-produced distilled spirits into the United States, importers must obtain a pre-import approval from TTB by submitting an ingredient list and quantitative formula for the product signed by the foreign manufacturer. This information can be submitted on TTB From 5100.51 or in letter form on the foreign manufacturer's letterhead.

ingredients or use production processes that would "change the character, composition, class or type" of a distilled spirit. TTB's application of this rule fluctuates over time. Nevertheless, a few generalizations can be drawn from TTB's long-term practices. Products of distillation alone (e.g., whiskey, brandy, vodka, rum) generally do not require a formula approval. On the other hand, TTB currently requires formula approvals for the following classes and types of distilled spirits:

- Liqueurs and cordials
- Gin, if botanicals are added after distillation
- Vodka subject to carbon filtration
- Flavored distilled spirits like flavored vodka, rum, brandy or whisky
- Any distilled spirit specialty product, which includes any distilled spirit that does not fit into a TTB-recognized class and type designation

In order to obtain a formula approval, a distiller must complete a formula application on TTB Form 5100.51, available at http://www.ttb.gov/forms/f510051.pdf. In boxes 6 and 7, the distiller must include a simplified recipe of a single batch that lists each ingredient along with a quantity or range of the ingredient's use in the batch, the alcohol content of any ingredients that contribute alcohol to the finished product, and a brief description of the production process. If the product contains flavors, the application should identify the TTB or ATF approval number for the flavor and include a Flavor Ingredient Data sheet, also called a FID sheet, completed by the flavor manufacturer that identifies the amount of certain ingredients that are subject to use limits in finished products.

TTB requires the submission of two executed formula applications to its Advertising, Labeling & Formulation Division (ALFD) located at its headquarters office in Washington, D.C. TTB does not impose fees on the submission of formula applications. Applications can be filed by mail, overnight delivery, or in person by the applicant or via several trade associations, law firms and consultants. In person delivery often saves time and reduces the risk that information might be lost as the application winds its way through the general mail and TTB's internal mail-routing system. During regular business hours, ALFD's customer service team is available for questions by industry members (202.927.8140).

Upon receiving a formula application, the assigned ALFD formulation specialist reviews it for compliance with federal law. Among the issues that a formulation specialist examines are whether: (1) the listed ingredients are generally recognized as safe (GRAS) under the standards enforced by the federal Food & Drug Administration, (2) the listed ingredients and processes can be used in the production of the class and type of distilled spirit identified on the formula application; and (3) TTB has approved the use of the particular ingredients and processes listed. Processing times for formula applications vary depending on ALFD's work-load, the complexities of the formula, and other factors. Currently, it can take ALFD three to four weeks to review a formula application and issue an approval or rejection. Delays of several months, however, are not uncommon. If ALFD issues a formula rejection, additional time is required for the distiller to modify and re-submit the formula until ALFD issues an approval. As a result, a formula rejection can be quite costly as a distiller cannot produce that distilled spirits product until ALFD approves the formula.

As with licensing, distillers must do their research before submitting a formula to TTB in order to reduce the risk of costly delays or flat-out rejections. Key research items include the class and type designation standards applicable to the distiller's product, whether or not the product's ingredients meet GRAS standards, and if TTB has a policy that addresses any ingredient or process to be used in the product's manufacture. Even if a distiller believes that a formula is a slam-dunk for approval, the distiller should incorporate sufficient time into its production plans to accommodate potential delays in ALFD's processing of that formula.

Resources

Distilled spirits permits
http://www.ttb.gov/foia/xls/spirits-producers-and-bottlers.xls

Distilled Spirits Laws and Regulations
http://www.ttb.gov/spirits/spirits_regs.shtml

The (CFR's) "styles of whiskey"
http://www.ttb.gov/spirits/chapter4.pdf

TTB statistics on distilling go to
www.ttb.gov then to "spirits" and then the "year".

State Alcohol Boards
http://www.ttb.gov/wine/control_board.shtml

C

Licensing

So You Want to Be a Micro-Distiller?

Then let's start with licensing issues

Robin Bowman

If your version of the American dream is to operate your own distillery, you will need more than just a good distilled spirits recipe to make that dream a reality. The production and sale of distilled spirits is heavily regulated by the federal government and the states, so getting into the distilling business takes thoughtful and thorough planning. This article addresses the first major phase of becoming a distiller, the licensing process.

Before you even start the license application process, you should consider some basic business matters:

What kind of business structure will best suit your needs - a sole proprietorship, a corporation, a limited liability entity?

Where will the distillery be located? Will local zoning, environmental and other ordinances accommodate your distillery?

What state business and tax registration requirements will apply to your business? Don't forget to apply for your Federal Employer Identification Number (FEIN).

What labor, employment, occupational safety or other regulatory standards will apply to your business

What type of distilled spirits do you intend to produce? What equipment, production methods and ingredients will your product(s) require?

Once you have your business model in mind, you will need to complete two license application processes, federal and state, in order to operate a distillery. At the federal level, the Alcohol & Tobacco Tax & Trade Bureau (TTB) handles licensing for alcohol production. Before a drop of distilled spirits can be made, all distillers, regardless of size, must apply to TTB for a federal basic permit and plant registration for their distilled spirits facility. TTB requires the submission of several application forms and a bond, but there is no application fee. You can review a basic distilled spirits plans application on TTB's website at http://www.ttb.gov/spirits/dsp_beverage_packet.shtml. Based on the distilled spirits products that you plan to produce and other factors, you may need to submit additional information and forms to TTB. As part of the application process, TTB also may require an on-site inspection of your distilling facility.

Simply submitting the required application forms to TTB is no guarantee that you will receive approval to operate a distillery. TTB has broad discretion in deciding whether to approve or deny a would-be distiller's application. Among the many factors that TTB considers, two of the most crucial are whether the distiller applicant or its owners have a criminal history or have violated a federal or state law relating to alcohol or its taxation.

You also should keep in mind that processing times can vary considerably depending on several factors, such as whether the would-be distiller already holds a federal brewer's notice or another type of basic permit, or if TTB identifies a skeleton in the applicant's closet. It often takes TTB several months to issue a basic permit and registration approval. Though you may find aspects of the application process confusing or frustrating, you should always deal with TTB in a respectful and reasonable manner. As you may recall from meeting your significant other's family for the first time, first impressions do matter and you will be dealing with TTB regularly once you start operations.

In addition to federal license procedures, you must apply to the alcohol beverage authority in the state where your distilling facility will be located for the type of license or permit that applies to your business operation. Several states have different licensing options for distillers based on production levels, use of in-state agricultural products, and other factors. States often require applicants to provide a copy of their federal basic permit. The fact that an applicant has a federal basic permit, however, is no guarantee that a state will issue the applicant a license or permit. States will conduct their own criminal background checks to see if the applicant and its owners have any cross-ownership relationships with other alcohol beverage licensees that prohibit the issuance of a state distiller's license. Restrictions that may prevent the issuance of a state distiller's license vary considerably among the states, so you are best served to identify these potential road-blocks early in your planning process. Also, many states require both a bond and payment of an application fee. To access information on the state alcohol beverage authorities and some basic license information, you can go to the National Conference of State Liquor Authorities website, http://www.ncsla.org/states.htm.

As you may have gathered, licensing a distillery is an involved and time-consuming process. Planning ahead and knowing the rules will help you reduce the risk of expensive delays and successfully navigate the complexities of federal and state licensing procedures.

D

Learn about COLA's

So You Want to Be a Micro-Distiller?

Then you need to learn about COLA's

Robin Bowman

As a micro-distiller, you want to distinguish your distilled spirit from competitors in the marketplace. So you've come up with a great idea for creating a distilled spirits label that is unique and sure to attract consumer attention. Before you invest a lot of money in expensive plates and reams of labels, you need to learn about the federal label approval process administered by the Alcohol & Tobacco Tax & Trade Bureau ("TTB") and how it might impact that unique label design you want to use.

Under the Federal Alcohol Administration Act, TTB requires alcohol beverage producers, including distillers, and importers to obtain pre-approval of label designs before the labels are used on alcohol beverages sold in interstate commerce (e.g., across state or national borders). Federal law requires label pre-approval for several reasons, including to ensure that labels are not misleading to consumers with regard to an alcohol beverage's class and type, quantity and method of manufacture and that they include the required mandatory information. Certain aspects of mandatory label information vary depending on the class and type of the distilled spirit, but the following elements are required for all domestically produced distilled spirits: brand name, alcohol content, net contents, class and type designation, name and address of the distiller/bottler/packer, and the government warning statement. Mandatory label information also is subject to rules governing font size, legibility and placement.

TTB administers label pre-approvals through its Certificate of Label Approval (COLA) system. To obtain a COLA for a distilled spirits product , the distilled spirits plant that bottles or packs the distilled spirit must submit two completed COLA forms bearing the entire proposed label design to the Advertising, Labeling and Formulation Division (ALFD), a division of TTB located at its headquarters in Washington, D.C. Copies of blank COLA forms, TTB Form 5100.31, can be found on TTB's website at http://www.ttb.gov/forms/ f510031.pdf. Certain information or items may need to accompany the COLA application. If the distilled spirits product requires a formula approval from TTB, the COLA application should include a copy of the approved formula so that TTB can determine if the class and type description and other information on the label is truthful and not misleading. If the label will be painted-on or applied with a translucent label to the bottle, the COLA application must include a real labeled bottle filled with appropriately colored liquid or a photograph or computer generated image of a filled, labeled bottle so that ALFD can examine the legibility and contrast of the mandatory label information. In addition, some COLA applications must include a request for a "distinctive liquor bottle approval" if the product will be bottled in an opaque or unusually shaped container that does not reveal the product's actual fill level.

COLA applications can be submitted to ALFD by mail, overnight delivery, in person delivery, either by the applicant or an agent such as a trade association, law firm or consultant, or electronically through TTB's COLAs Online system. In person delivery or use of the COLAs Online system are the preferred options for submitting COLAs as they reduce the risk that COLA forms or key information may be lost or destroyed in delivery. Processing times for COLAs by ALFD can vary from about fourteen days to several weeks depending on the complexity of the label design, the back-log of applications and whether the COLA is rejected. In special circumstances, a COLA applicant can request expedited review of a COLA if the applicant presents ALFD with a clear written request describing the reasons the applicant needs expedited review along with supporting documentation for the request.

ALFD can approve, reject or qualify a COLA application. If ALFD rejects a COLA application, it provides the applicant with an explanation of the reason(s) for rejection. The applicant then may resubmit corrected COLA application forms, including revised labels if necessary, along with ALFD's rejection sheet. ALFD also may issue a COLA approval with qualifications, such a COLA that only be used for a limited period and for a maximum amount of product (commonly referred to as a "use-up" COLA) or a COLA approved subject to specific restrictions. If an applicant believes that ALFD rejected or qualified the use of a COLA in error, the applicant can seek to persuade ALFD to change its position through an informal review process. Many labeling disputes are resolved through this informal review process between ALFD and COLA applicants or their attorney or consultant. TTB has a formal appeals procedure for COLA disputes, but the length of time required to complete this process limits its usefulness.

Having an approved COLA for a distilled spirit allows the distiller or bottler to bottle or pack that product in containers bearing the approved label for sale in interstate commerce. If a distilled spirit will be sold only within the state where it is bottled and not in interstate commerce, TTB requires the submission of a COLA application marked in box 18 to request a certificate of exemption from label approval. All exemptions issued by TTB bear the qualification "For sale in [state] only."

It is important that a distiller or bottler only uses those labels that have an approved COLA. If an approved label design is modified, a new COLA must be obtained unless the change fits within the limited exceptions allowed by TTB. Label changes that can be done without a new COLA application are listed on the back of TTB Form 5100.31. Using an unapproved label can have serious consequences. TTB possesses broad powers to punish distillers for bottling prior to obtaining a COLA, including the authority to first suspend, then revoke, a distiller's federal basic permit, which is the federal license needed to distill. TTB often compromises mislabeling charges for monetary fines, which can be quite large in extreme circumstances. On the other hand, an approved COLA generally precludes TTB from punishing a distiller that is using an approved label if that label accurately reflects the contents of the container. TTB may revoke a previously-approved COLA, but the revocation procedure permits the continued use of the label until TTB completes the revocation process, which might take a year or longer if the COLA holder exercises its rights to contest and appeal the revocation.

To avoid costly problems, it is important to keep the following points in mind. First, when planning any product launch, anticipate the formula and COLA processes and build in plenty of time for these applications into your schedule. Second, check and double check how TTB labeling legalities might impact your label design. Third, to avoid wasting valuable time and money, do not order production labels until you have secured COLA approval from TTB. If you follow these rules, you'll find label pre-approval to be simply a necessary process to complete rather than a potential business disaster.

Robin J. Bowen is Alcohol Beverage Counsel at the law firm of McDermott Will & Emery LLP, based in the firm's Washington, D.C. office. She is a member of the firm's Alcohol Beverages and Products Group where her practice focuses on regulatory, distribution and customs issues facing the alcohol beverage industry.

E

CRF (Code of Federal Regulations) Standards of Identity

Code of Federal Regulations (CFR)

§ 5.22 The standards of identity.

Standards of identity for the several classes and types of distilled spirits set forth in this section shall be as follows (see also §5.35, class and type):

(a) Class 1; neutral spirits or alcohol. "Neutral spirits" or "alcohol" are distilled spirits produced from any material at or above 190° proof, and, if bottled, bottled at not less than 80° proof.

(1) "Vodka" is neutral spirits so distilled, or so treated after distillation with charcoal or other materials, as to be without distinctive character, aroma, taste, or color.

(2) "Grain spirits" are neutral spirits distilled from a fermented mash of grain and stored in oak containers.

(b) Class 2; whiskey. "Whiskey" is an alcoholic distillate from a fermented mash of grain produced at less than 190° proof in such manner that the distillate possesses the taste, aroma, and characteristics generally attributed to whiskey, stored in oak containers (except that corn whiskey need not be so stored), and bottled at not less than 80° proof, and also includes mixtures of such distillates for which no specific standards of identity are prescribed.

(1)(i) "Bourbon whiskey," "rye whiskey," "wheat whiskey," "malt whiskey," or "rye malt whiskey" is whiskey produced at not exceeding 160° proof from a fermented mash of not less than 51 percent corn, rye, wheat, malted barley, or malted rye grain, respectively, and stored at not more than 125° proof in charred new oak containers; and also includes mixtures of such whiskies of the same type.

(ii) "Corn whiskey" is whiskey produced at not exceeding 160° proof from a fermented mash of not less than 80 percent corn grain, and if stored in oak containers stored at not more than 125° proof in used or uncharred new oak containers and not subjected in any manner to treatment with charred wood; and also includes mixtures of such whiskey.

(iii) Whiskies conforming to the standards prescribed in paragraphs (b)(1)(i) and (ii) of this section, which have been stored in the type of oak containers prescribed, for a period of 2 years or more shall be further designated as "straight;" for example, "straight bourbon whiskey," "straight corn whiskey," and whiskey conforming to the standards prescribed in paragraph (b)(1)(i) of this section, except that it was produced from a fermented mash of less than 51 percent of any one type of grain, and stored for a period of 2 years or more in charred new oak containers shall be designated merely as "straight whiskey." No other whiskies may be designated "straight." "Straight whiskey" includes mixtures of straight whiskies of the same type produced in the same State.

(2) "Whiskey distilled from bourbon (rye, wheat, malt, or rye malt) mash" is whiskey produced in the United States at not exceeding 160° proof from a fermented mash of not less than 51 percent corn, rye, wheat, malted barley, or malted rye grain, respectively, and stored in used oak containers; and also includes mixtures of such whiskies of the same type. Whiskey conforming to the standard of identity for corn whiskey must be designated corn whiskey.

(3) "Light whiskey" is whiskey produced in the United States at more than 160° proof, on or after January 26, 1968, and stored in used or uncharred new oak containers; and also includes mixtures of such whiskies. If "light whiskey" is mixed with less than 20 percent of straight whiskey on a proof gallon basis, the mixture shall be designated "blended light whiskey" (light whiskey— a blend).

(4) "Blended whiskey" (whiskey blend) is a mixture which contains straight whiskey or a blend of straight whiskies at not less than 20 percent on a proof gallon basis, excluding alcohol derived from added harmless coloring, flavoring or blending materials, and, separately, or in combination, whiskey or neutral spirits. A blended whiskey containing not less than 51 percent on a proof gallon basis of one of the types of straight whiskey shall be further designated by that specific type of straight whiskey; for example, "blended rye whiskey" (rye whiskey— a blend).

(5)(i) "A blend of straight whiskies" (blended straight whiskies) is a mixture of straight whiskies which does not conform to the standard of identify for "straight whiskey." Products so designated may contain harmless coloring, flavoring, or blending materials as set forth in 27 CFR 5.23(a).

(ii) "A blend of straight whiskies" (blended straight whiskies) consisting entirely of one of the types of straight whiskey, and not conforming to the standard for straight whiskey, shall be further designated by that specific type of straight whiskey; for example, "a blend of straight rye whiskies" (blended straight rye whiskies). "A blend of straight whiskies" consisting entirely of one of the types of straight whiskey shall include straight whiskey of the same type which was produced in the same State or by the same proprietor within the same State, provided that such whiskey contains harmless coloring, flavoring, or blending materials as stated in 27 CFR 5.23(a).

(iii) The harmless coloring, flavoring, or blending materials allowed under this section shall not include neutral spirits or alcohol in their original state. Neutral spirits or alcohol may only appear in a "blend of straight whiskies" or in a "blend of straight whiskies consisting entirely of one of the types of straight whiskey" as a vehicle for recognized flavoring of blending material.

(6) "Spirit whiskey" is a mixture of neutral spirits and not less than 5 percent on a proof gallon basis of whiskey, or straight whiskey, or straight whiskey and whiskey, if the straight whiskey component is less than 20 percent on a proof gallon basis.

(7) "Scotch whiskey" is whiskey which is a distinctive product of Scotland, manufactured in Scotland in compliance with the laws of the United Kingdom regulating the manufacture of Scotch whiskey for consumption in the United Kingdom: Provided, That if such product is a mixture of whiskies, such mixture is "blended Scotch whiskey" (Scotch whiskey— a blend).

(8) "Irish whiskey" is whiskey which is a distinctive product of Ireland, manufactured either in the Republic of Ireland or in Northern Ireland, in compliance with their laws regulating the manufacture of Irish whiskey for home consumption: Provided, That if such product is a mixture of whiskies, such mixture is "blended Irish whiskey" (Irish whiskey— a blend).

(9) "Canadian whiskey" is whiskey which is a distinctive product of Canada, manufactured in Canada in compliance with the laws of Canada regulating the manufacture of Canadian whiskey for consumption in Canada: Provided, That if such product is a mixture of whiskies, such mixture is "blended Canadian whiskey" (Canadian whiskey— a blend).

(c) Class 3; gin. "Gin" is a product obtained by original distillation from mash, or by redistillation of distilled spirits, or by mixing neutral spirits, with or over juniper berries and other aromatics, or with or over extracts derived from infusions, percolations, or maceration of such materials, and includes mixtures of gin and neutral spirits. It shall derive its main characteristic flavor from juniper berries and be bottled at not less than 80° proof. Gin produced exclusively by original distillation or by redistillation may be further designated as "distilled." "Dry gin" (London dry gin), "Geneva gin" (Hollands gin), and "Old Tom gin" (Tom gin) are types of gin known under such designations.

(d) Class 4; brandy. "Brandy" is an alcoholic distillate from the fermented juice, mash, or wine of fruit, or from the residue thereof, produced at less than 190° proof in such manner that the distillate possesses the taste, aroma, and characteristics generally attributed to the product, and bottled at not less than 80° proof. Brandy, or mixtures thereof, not conforming to any of the standards in paragraphs (d) (1) through (8) of this section shall be designated as "brandy," and such designation shall be immediately followed by a truthful and adequate statement of composition.

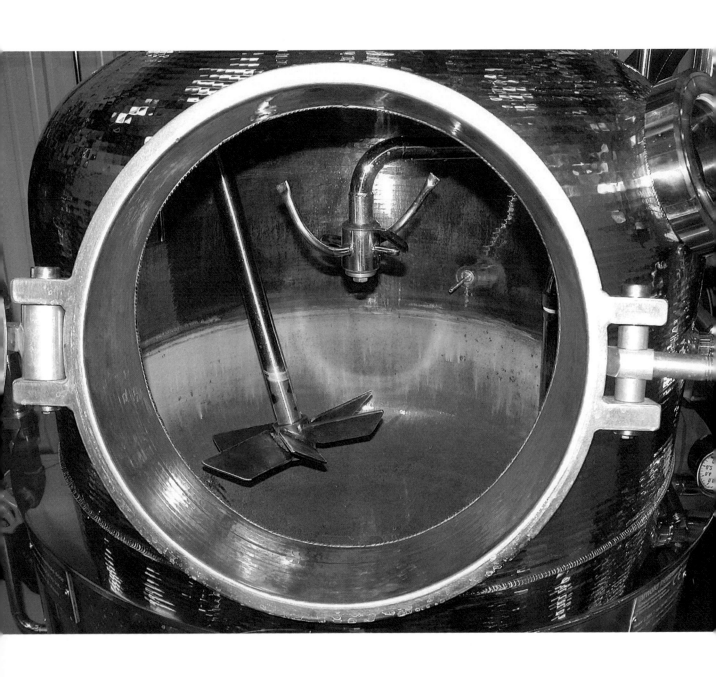

(1) "Fruit brandy" is brandy distilled solely from the fermented juice or mash of whole, sound, ripe fruit, or from standard grape, citrus, or other fruit wine, with or without the addition of not more than 20 percent by weight of the pomace of such juice or wine, or 30 percent by volume of the lees of such wine, or both (calculated prior to the addition of water to facilitate fermentation or distillation). Fruit brandy shall include mixtures of such brandy with not more than 30 percent (calculated on a proof gallon basis) of lees brandy. Fruit brandy, derived from grapes, shall be designated as "grape brandy" or "brandy," except that in the case of brandy (other than neutral brandy, pomace brandy, marc brandy or grappa brandy) distilled from the fermented juice, mash, or wine of grapes, or the residue thereof, which has been stored in oak containers for less than 2 years, the statement of class and type shall be immediately preceded, in the same size and kind of type, by the word "immature." Fruit brandy, other than grape brandy, derived from one variety of fruit, shall be designated by the word "brandy" qualified by the name of such fruit (for example, "peach brandy"), except that "apple brandy" may be designated "applejack." Fruit brandy derived from more than one variety of fruit shall be designated as "fruit brandy" qualified by a truthful and adequate statement of composition.

(2) "Cognac," or "Cognac (grape) brandy," is grape brandy distilled in the Cognac region of France, which is entitled to be so designated by the laws and regulations of the French Government.

(3) "Dried fruit brandy" is brandy that conforms to the standard for fruit brandy except that it has been derived from sound, dried fruit, or from the standard wine of such fruit. Brandy derived from raisins, or from raisin wine, shall be designated as "raisin brandy." Other brandies shall be designated in the same manner as fruit brandy from the corresponding variety or varieties of fruit except that the name of the fruit shall be qualified by the word "dried."

(4) "Lees brandy" is brandy distilled from the lees of standard grape, citrus, or other fruit wine, and shall be designated as "lees brandy," qualified by the name of the fruit from which such lees are derived.

(5) "Pomace brandy," or "marc brandy," is brandy distilled from the skin and pulp of sound, ripe grapes, citrus or other fruit, after the withdrawal of the juice or wine therefrom, and shall be designated as "pomace brandy," or "marc brandy," qualified by the name of the fruit from which derived. Grape pomace brandy may be designated as "grappa" or "grappa brandy."

(6) "Residue brandy" is brandy distilled wholly or in part from the fermented residue of fruit or wine, and shall be designated as "residue brandy" qualified by the name of the fruit from which derived. Brandy distilled wholly or in part from residue materials which conforms to any of the standards set forth in paragraphs (d) (1), (3), (4), and (5) of this section may, regardless of such fact, be designated "residue brandy," but the use of such designation shall be conclusive, precluding any later change of designation.

(7) "Neutral brandy" is brandy produced at more than 170° proof and shall be designated in accordance with the standards in this paragraph, except that the designation

shall be qualified by the word "neutral"; for example, "neutral citrus residue brandy."

(8) "Substandard brandy" shall bear as a part of its designation the word "substandard," and shall include:

(i) Any brandy distilled from fermented juice, mash, or wine having a volatile acidity, calculated as acetic acid and exclusive of sulfur dioxide, in excess of 0.20 gram per 100 cubic centimeters (20 °C.); measurements of volatile acidity shall be calculated exclusive of water added to facilitate distillation.

(ii) Any brandy which has been distilled from unsound, moldy, diseased, or decomposed juice, mash, wine, lees, pomace, or residue, or which shows in the finished product any taste, aroma, or characteristic associated with products distilled from such material.

(e) Class 5; blended applejack. "Blended applejack" (applejack blend) is a mixture which contains at least 20 percent of apple brandy (applejack) on a proof gallon basis, stored in oak containers for not less than 2 years, and not more than 80 percent of neutral spirits on a proof gallon basis if such mixture at the time of bottling is not less than 80° proof.

(f) Class 6; rum. "Rum" is an alcoholic distillate from the fermented juice of sugar cane, sugar cane syrup, sugar cane molasses, or other sugar cane by-products, produced at less than 190° proof in such manner that the distillate possesses the taste, aroma and characteristics generally attributed to rum, and bottled at not less than 80° proof; and also includes mixtures solely of such distillates.

(g) Class 7; Tequila. "Tequila" is an alcoholic distillate from a fermented mash derived principally from the Agave Tequilana Weber ("blue" variety), with or without additional fermentable substances, distilled in such a manner that the distillate possesses the taste, aroma, and characteristics generally attributed to Tequila and bottled at not less than 80° proof, and also includes mixtures solely of such distillates. Tequila is a distinctive product of Mexico, manufactured in Mexico in compliance with the laws of Mexico regulating the manufacture of Tequila for consumption in that country.

(h) Class 8; cordials and liqueurs. Cordials and liqueurs are products obtained by mixing or redistilling distilled spirits with or over fruits, flowers, plants, or pure juices therefrom, or other natural flavoring materials, or with extracts derived from infusions, percolation, or maceration of such materials, and containing sugar, dextrose, or levulose, or a combination thereof, in an amount not less than 21/2 percent by weight of the finished product.

(1) "Sloe gin" is a cordial or liqueur with the main characteristic flavor derived from sloe berries.

(2) "Rye liqueur," "bourbon liqueur" (rye, bourbon cordial) are liqueurs, bottled at not less than 60° proof, in which not less than 51 percent, on a proof gallon basis, of the distilled spirits used are, respectively, rye or bourbon whiskey, straight rye or straight bourbon whiskey, or whiskey distilled from a rye or bourbon mash, and which possess

a predominant characteristic rye or bourbon flavor derived from such whiskey. Wine, if used, must be within the 21/2 percent limitation provided in §5.23 for coloring, flavoring, and blending materials.

(3) "Rock and rye," "rock and bourbon," "rock and brandy," "rock and rum" are liqueurs, bottled at not less than 48° proof, in which, in the case of rock and rye and rock and bourbon, not less than 51 percent, on a proof gallon basis, of the distilled spirits used are, respectively, rye or bourbon whiskey, straight rye or straight bourbon whiskey, or whiskey distilled from a rye or bourbon mash, and, in the case of rock and brandy and rock and rum, the distilled spirits used are all grape brandy or rum, respectively; containing rock candy or sugar syrup, with or without the addition of fruit, fruit juices, or other natural flavoring materials, and possessing, respectively, a predominant characteristic rye, bourbon, brandy, or rum flavor derived from the distilled spirits used. Wine, if used, must be within the 21/2 percent limitation provided in §5.23 for harmless coloring, flavoring, and blending materials.

(4) "Rum liqueur," "gin liqueur," "brandy liqueur," are liqueurs, bottled at not less than 60 proof, in which the distilled spirits used are entirely rum, gin, or brandy, respectively, and which possess, respectively, a predominant characteristic rum, gin, or brandy flavor derived from the distilled spirits used. In the case of brandy liqueur, the type of brandy must be stated in accordance with §5.22(d), except that liqueurs made entirely with grape brandy may be designated simply as "brandy liqueur." Wine, if used, must be within the 21/2 percent limitation provided for in §5.23 for harmless coloring, flavoring, and blending materials.

(5) The designation of a cordial or liqueur may include the word "dry" if the sugar, dextrose, or levulose, or a combination thereof, are less than 10 percent by weight of the finished product.

(6) Cordials and liqueurs shall not be designated as "distilled" or "compound."

(i) Class 9; flavored brandy, flavored gin, flavored rum, flavored vodka, and flavored whiskey. "Flavored brandy, "flavored gin," "flavored rum," "flavored vodka," and "flavored whiskey," are brandy, gin, rum vodka, and whiskey, respectively, to which have been added natural flavoring materials, with or without the addition of sugar, and bottled at not less than 60° proof. The name of the predominant flavor shall appear as a part of the designation. If the finished product contains more than 21/2 percent by volume of wine, the kinds and precentages by volume of wine must be stated as a part of the designation, except that a flavored brandy may contain an additional 121/2 percent by volume of wine, without label disclosure, if the additional wine is derived from the particular fruit corresponding to the labeled flavor of the product.

(j) Class 10; imitations. Imitations shall bear, as a part of the designation thereof, the word "imitation" and shall include the following:

(1) Any class or type of distilled spirits to which has been added coloring or flavoring material of such nature as to cause the resultant product to simulate any other class or type of distilled spirits;

(2) Any class or type of distilled spirits (other than distilled spirits required under §5.35 to bear a distinctive or fanciful name and a truthful and adequate statement of composition) to which has been added flavors considered to be artificial or imitation. In determining whether a flavor is artificial or imitation, recognition will be given to what is considered to be "good commercial practice" in the flavor manufacturing industry;

(3) Any class of type of distilled spirits (except cordials, liqueurs and specialties marketed under labels which do not indicate or imply, that a particular class or type of distilled spirits was used in the manufacture thereof) to which has been added any whiskey essense, brandy essence, rum essence, or similar essence or extract which simulates or enhances, or is used by the trade or in the particular product to simulate or enhance, the characteristics of any class or type of distilled spirits;

(4) Any type of whiskey to which beading oil has been added;

(5) Any rum to which neutral spirits or distilled spirits other than rum have been added;

(6) Any brandy made from distilling material to which has been added any amount of sugar other than the kind and amount of sugar expressly authorized in the production of standard wine; and

(7) Any brandy to which neutral spirits or distilled spirits other than brandy have been added, except that this provision shall not apply to any product conforming to the standard of identity for blended applejack.

(k) Class 11; geographical designations. (1) Geographical names for distinctive types of distilled spirits (other than names found by the appropriate TTB officer under paragraph (k)(2) of this section to have become generic) shall not be applied to distilled spirits produced in any other place than the particular region indicated by the name, unless (i) in direct conjunction with the name there appears the word "type" or the word "American" or some other adjective indicating the true place of production, in lettering substantially as conspicuous as such name, and (ii) the distilled spirits to which the name is applied conform to the distilled spirits of that particular region. The following are examples of distinctive types of distilled spirits with geographical names that have not become generic: Eau de Vie de Dantzig (Danziger Goldwasser), Ojen, Swedish punch. Geographical names for distinctive types of distilled spirits shall be used to designate only distilled spirits conforming to the standard of identity, if any, for such type specified in this section, or if no such standard is so specified, then in accordance with the trade understanding of that distinctive type.

(2) Only such geographical names for distilled spirits as the appropriate TTB officer finds have by usage and common knowledge lost their geographical significance to such extent that they have become generic shall be deemed to have become generic. Examples at London dry gin, Geneva (Hollands) gin.

(3) Geographical names that are not names for distinctive types of distilled spirits, and that have not become generic, shall not be applied to distilled spirits produced in any

other place than the particular place or region indicated in the name. Examples are Cognac, Armagnac, Greek brandy, Pisco brandy, Jamaica rum, Puerto Rico rum, Demerara rum.

(4) The words "Scotch," "Scots" "Highland," or "Highlands" and similar words connoting, indicating, or commonly associated with Scotland, shall not be used to designate any product not wholly produced in Scotland.

(l) Class 12; products without geographical designations but distinctive of a particular place. (1) The whiskies of the types specified in paragraphs (b) (1), (4), (5), and (6) of this section are distinctive products of the United States and if produced in a foreign country shall be designated by the applicable designation prescribed in such paragraphs, together with the words "American type" or the words "produced (distilled, blended) in __," the blank to be filled in with the name of the foreign country: Provided, That the word "bourbon" shall not be used to describe any whiskey or whiskey-based distilled spirits not produced in the United States. If whiskey of any of these types is composed in part of whiskey or whiskies produced in a foreign country there shall be stated, on the brand label, the percentage of such whiskey and the country of origin thereof.

(2) The name for other distilled spirits which are distinctive products of a particular place or country, an example is Habanero, shall not be given to the product of any other place or country unless the designation for such product includes the word "type" or an adjective such as "American," or the like, clearly indicating the true place of production. The provision for place of production shall not apply to designations which by usage and common knowledge have lost their geographical significance to such an extent that the appropriate TTB officer finds they have become generic. Examples are Slivovitz, Zubrovka, Aquavit, Arrack, and Kirschwasser.

F

Down & Dirty Business Plan

Assumption One You will keep you day job during planning and building of a craft distillery. (One-Three years)

Assumption Two The first year you will be spent thinking about financing the distillery. Year two, finding a location then obtaining all the permits necessary to build a craft distillery. Next obtain City, Country Use permits to build a distillery. Then order your equipment. After the distilling equipment is installed apply for a DSP from TTB. Finally obtain COLA and Label approval for products.

Assumption Three It will cost over $350,000 to open a distillery capable of producing 3,000 to 5,000 cases / year.

Assumption Four Income from your first year of production will come from distilling gin and then whiskey. (Gin take two days to produce from NGS. Malt whiskey should be aged from six months to two years.)

EXPENSE	COST
YEAR TWO—THE BUILD OUT	
BUILDING IMPROVEMENTS	
Electrical, Plumbing, Fire Protection, General Construction	$50,000
One year rent—$2,500 x 12	$30,000
BUILD OUT EXPENSES	$80,000
BREWING EQUIPMENT (NEW & USED)	
Boiler, Mash Tun, Two Fermentation Vessels to create a whiskey wash	$70,000
DISTILLING EQUIPMENT	
350 Gallon Wash Still	$35,000
100 gallon Spirits Still	$12,000
Pumps, Hoses and Filtration System	$3,500
Hydrometers, Thermometers & Ebulliometer	$600
Office furniture, computers, phones	$4,000
Legal Fees, Trademark etc.	$5,000
EQUIPMENT	$60,100
SUBTOTAL	$210,100
Reserve in bank account for unexpected expenses	$47,000
TOTAL CASH OUT	$257,100
YEAR THREE—PRODUCTION	
ANNUAL OUTPUT / CASES / $ PER CASE	
Gin/2,000/$260	$520,000
Whiskey/660/$350	$115,500
TOTAL RETAIL SALES	$635,500
less 50% to wholesale retailer	-$317,750
GROSS INCOME	$317,750
Federal Excise Tax	-$60,000
Direct cost of goods	-$83,500
Marketing	-$56,000
Rent, utilities, insurance, travel	-$61,000
END OF YEAR NET INCOME	$57,250

Many distilleries are grossing between $10 and 30,000/mo. in sales from tasting rooms, tours and gift shops.

[pictured above— Panther Distillery tasting room in Minnesota]

G

Resources

Equipment
Recommended Reading
US and Canada Distilleries

Over 350 DSP licenses exist, of which 151 are craft distilleries. The rest of the companies on the list are industrial distilleries, rectifiers and importers. If someone claims to be a distillery check their website. If it doesn't show a still most likely they don't own one— they purchase NGS and repackaging the products.

GOVERNMENT WEBSITES

Distilled spirits permits http://www.ttb.gov/spirits/index.shtml

Distilled spirits Laws and Regulations http://www.ttb.gov/spirits/spirits_regs.shtml

(CFR's) "Styles of whiskey" http://www.ttb.gov/spirits/chapter4.pdf

TTB statistics on distilling www.ttb.gov/
then to "spirits" then to the "year."

State Alcohol Boards
http://www.ttb.gov/wine/control_board.shtml

TRADE MAGAZINES

Beverage Industry, www.bevindustry.com

Distiller, www.distilling.com

Drink Me Magazine, drinkmemag.com

Imbibe, www.imbibemagazine.com

K&L Spirits Journal, spiritsjournal.klwines.com

Mutineer Magazine, www.mutineermagazine.com

The Brewer & Distiller, www.ibd.org/uk

Whiskey Advocate, www.whiskeyadvocate.com

Whiskey Magazine, www.whiskeymag.com

ANNUAL TRADE EVENTS

American Distilling Institute Trade Show www.distilling.com

Craft Spirits Carnival, www.craftspiritscarnival.com

Manhattan Cocktail Classic, www.manhattancocktailclassic.com

Ministry of Rum, www.ministryofrum.com

New York Bar Show www.newyorkbarshow.com

Tales of the Cocktail www.talesofthecocktails.com

Whiskeyfest www.whiskeyadvocate.com

Whiskey Live www.whiskeylive.com

Whiskies of the World www.whiskiesoftheworld.com

Wine & Spirit Wholesalers of America www.wswa.org

Worldwide Distilled Spirits Conference www.distillingconferences.com

DISTILLING EQUIPMENT MANUFACTURERS

Adrian Edelbrande GmbH
208-455-8386
www.koenigdistillery.com

Artisan Copperworks
403-795-0602
www.artisancopperworks.com

Bavarian-Holstein Partners
310-391-1091
www.potstills.com

Carl Distilleries
215-242-6806
www.brewing-distilling.com

Chalvignac Prulho Distillation
33-6-22-15-22-15
www.groupe-novtech.com

Foothill Rocks Import + Export
250-503-4731

Forsyth
44-1340-831-787
www.forsyth.com

Hillbilly Stills
270-334-3400
www.hillbillystills.com

Hoga Company
351-226-062430
www.hogacompany.com

Kothe Distilling Technologies
571-278-1313
www.kothe-distilling.com

Oregon Copper Works
541-485-9845
www.oregoncopperbowl.com

Vendome Copper & Brass Works
501-587-1930
www.vendome.com

WHISKEY DISTILLERIES OF NOTE

ARKANSAS
Rock Town Distillery
arkansaslightning.com

CALIFORNIA
1512 Spirits
1512spirits.com

American Craft Whiskey Distillery
craftdistillers.com

Anchor Brewing & Distilling
anchorbrewing.com

Ballast Point Spirits
ballastpoint.com

Fog's End Distillery
fogsenddistillery.com

Lost Spirits Distillery
lostspiritsdistillery.net

St. George Spirits
stgeorgespirits.com

Valley Spirits
drinkvalleyspirits.com

COLORADO
Breckenridge Distillery
breckenridgedistillery.com

Leopold Bros.
leopoldbros.com

Peach Street Distillers
peachstreetdistillers.com

Stranahan's Colorado Whiskey
stranahans.com

FLORIDA
Florida Farm Distillers
palmridgereserve.com

ILLINOIS
Few Spirits
fewspirits.com

Koval Distillery
koval-distillery.com

IOWA
Mississippi River Distilling Company
mrdistilling.com

KANSAS
Dark Horse Distillery
dhdistillery.com

KENTUCKY
Alltech Brewing & Distilling Co.
alltech.com

MB Roland Distillery
mbrdistillery.com

Limestone Branch Distillery
limestonebranch.com

Silver Trail Distillery
lblmoonshine.com

MASSACHUSETTS
Berkshire Mountain Distillers
berkshiremountaindistillers.com

Nashoba Distillery
nashobawinery.com

Triple Eight Distillery
ciscobrewers.com

MICHIGAN
Journeyman Distillery
journeymandistillery.com

New Holland Brewing Co.
newhollandbrew.com

MINNESOTA
Panther Distillery
pantherdistillery.com

MISSISSIPPI
Cathead Distillery
catheadvodka.com

MISSOURI
Copper Run Distillery
copperrundistillery.com

Square One Brewery and Distillery
squareonebrewery.com

MONTANA
Flathead Distillers
flatheaddistillers.com

Glacier Distilling Co.
glacierdistilling.com

Headframe Spirits
headframespirits.com

Ridge Distillery
ridgedistillery.com

Rough Stock Distillery
montanawhiskey.com

Whistling Andy
whistlingandy.com

Willie's Distillery
williesdistillery.com

NEW MEXICO
Santa Fe Spirits
santafespirits.com

NEW YORK
Albany Distilling
albanydistilling.com

Catskill Distilling Co.
catskilldistilling.com

Finger Lakes Distilling
fingerlakesdistilling.com

Hillrock Estate Distillery & Malthouse
hillrockdistillery.com

Kings County Distillery
kingscountydistillery.com

Tuthilltown Spirits Distillery
Tuthilltown.com

NORTH CAROLINA
Asheville Distilling Co.
troyandsons.com

Blue Ridge Distilling Co.
blueridgedistilling.com

OHIO
Ernest Scarano Distillery
esdistillery.com

Indian Creek Distillery
staleymillfarmanddistillery.com

Middle West Spirits
middlewestspirits.com

Red Eagle Spirits
redeaglespirits.com

Tom's Foolery
tomsfoolery.com

Watershed Distillery
watersheddistillery.com

OREGON
Bull Run Distilling
bullrundistillery.com

House Spirits Distillery
housespirits.com

Rogue House of Spirits
roguespirits.com

RHODE ISLAND
Newport Distilling Company
thomastewrums.com

Sons of Liberty
solspirits.com

SOUTH CAROLINA
Dark Corner Distillery
darkcornerdistillery.com

TENNESSEE
Corsair Artisan Distillery
corsairartisan.com

Ole Smoky Distillery
olesmokymoonshine.com

Prichard's Distillery
prichardsdistillery.com

Short Mountain Distillery
shortmountaindistillery.com

Tenn South Distillery
tennsouthdistillery.com

TEXAS
Balcones Distilling
balconesdistilling.com

Garrison Brothers Distillery
garrisonbros.com

Ranger CreekBrewing & Distillery
drinkrangercreek.com

Rebecca Creek Distillery
rebeccacreekdistillery.com

Yellow Rose Distilling
yellowrosedistilling.com

UTAH
High West Distillery
highwest.com

VIRGINIA
Belmont Farms
virginiamoonshine.com
virginiawhiskey.com

Catoctin Creek Distilling Co.
catoctincreekdistilling.com

Copper Fox Distillery
copperfox.biz

Virgilina Distilling Co.

Virginia Distillery Co.
vadistillery.com

WASHINGTON
Bainbridge Organic Distillers
bainbridgedistillers.com

Oola Distillery
ooladistillery.com

Skip Rock Distillers
skiprockdistillers.com

Woodinville Whiskey Co.
woodinvillewhiskeyco.com

WEST VIRGINIA
Pinchgut Hollow Distillery
PinchgutHollowDistillery.com

Smooth Ambler Spirits
smoothambler.com

West Virginia Distilling
mountainmoonshine.com

WISCONSIN
45th Parallel Spirits
45thparallelspirits.com

Great Lakes Distillery
greatlakesdistillery.com

Yahara Bay Distillers
yaharabay.com

CANADA
66 Gilead Distillery
66gileaddistillery.com

Kittling Ridge Wine & Spirits
fortycreekwhisky.com

LB Distillers
luckybastard.ca

Shelter Point Distillery
shelterpointdistillery.com

Still Waters Distillery
stillwatersdistillery.com

Yukon Spirits
yukonbeer.com

EUROPE
AUSTRIA
Roggenhof Haider
roggenhof.at

DENMARK
Braunstein
braunstein.dk

Stauning
stauningwhisky.dk

FRANCE
Warenghem distillerie
warenghem.com

Kaerilis Ltd.
kaeriliswhisky.com

Celtic Whiskey Companie
glannarmor.com

GERMANY
Slyrs
slyrs.de

Coillmor
coillmor.com

SWEDEN
Mackmyra
mackmyra.se

SWITZERLAND
Rugen and Saentis Malt
www.rugenbraeu.ch/de/distillery.html

UK
The London Distillery
thelondondistillerycompany.com

RECOMMENDED READING

TECHNICAL DISTILLING BOOKS:

1. *Whiskey: Technology, Production and Marketing*, edited by Inge Russell, Charles Bamforth, and Graham Stewart; ISBN 9780126692020. (Highly recommended).

2. *Fermented Beverage Production*, Second Edition (paperback); by Andrew G.H. Lea, editor and John R. Piggott, editor.

3. *Fundametal of Distillery Practice*, by Herman F. Willkie and Joseph A. Prochaska; published by Joseph E. Segram & Sons; 1943.

4. *The Science and Technology of Whiskies*, edited by J. R. Piggott, R. E. Duncan, & R. Sharp. ISBN 9780582044289.

5. *Distilled Beverage Flavour*, edited by J.R. Piggott and A. Patterson; Ellis Horwood Series in Food Science and Technology. (This isn't for beginners).

6. *The Alcohol Textbook*, is sold out. Order the CD http://www.murtagh.com/textbook-4-CD.html

7. *The Whiskey Distilleries of the United Kingdom*, by Alfred Barnard; 1887. This was reprinted in 1969 and again more recently.

8. *The Manufacture of Whiskey and Plain Spirit*, by J.A. Nettleton; 1913 and his 8 other books published from 1881 to 1897.

9. *Illicit Scotch*, by S.W. Sillett; 1965.

10. *The Scotch Whiskey Industry Record*, by H. Charles Craig; 1994 ISBN 0 9522646 0 9.

BOOKS FOR THE START UP DISTILLER:

1. *Making Pure Corn Whiskey*, by Ian Smiley. Ian also wrote the how to section of this book. ISBN 0-9686292-1-0; www.home-distilling.com

2. *The Complete Distiller*, by Mike McCaw; www.amphora-society.com

3. *Alcohol Distiller's Handbook*, Desert Publications; info@deltapress.com

4. *Distiller's Manual*, available from www.qualitybooks.com. Old but a good "history" read.

5. *Practical Distiller*, Samual M'Harry; www.raudins.com/brewbooks (http://www.raudins.com/brewbooks). Reprint of 1809 distilling manual.

6. *Cider*, A Story Publishing Book; 800-793-9396

7. *Whiskey*, by Michael Jackson; 0-7894-9710-7; www.dk.com.

8. *Moonshine Made Simple*, by Byron Ford; byronfordbooks@hotmail.com

9. *How to Brew*, by John Palmer; www.beertown.org.

H

Quiz

1 When setting up a new whiskey distillery, the minimum investment in mashing and fermentation equipment is:

[a] $75,000 for a 1,100-gallon brewery

[b] $110,000 for a 3,000-gallon brewery

[c] $30,000 because whiskey-mashing equipment is less complex and therefore less expensive than brewing equipment

[d] $0 because a start-up whiskey distillery can contract a local microbrewery to produce their wash for them

2 Starch is:

[a] a type of sugar

[b] a type of alcohol

[c] a long chain of sugar molecules

[d] an enzyme

3 The most widely used malted grain for producing whiskey is:

[a] barley

[b] corn

[c] rye

[d] wheat

4 The source-water mineral that's the most destructive to the mashing enzymes is:

[a] calcium

[b] magnesium

[c] iron

[d] lead

5 The optimum pH range for mashing enzymes to convert starches to sugars is:

[a] 7.4 – 7.8

[b] 3.3 – 3.7

[c] 5.2 – 5.5

[d] 5.8 – 6.0

6 To lower pH in a mash water:

[a] water salts are added

[b] acid is added

[c] alkali is added

[d] all of the above

7 The optimum temperature range for starch conversion in
a whiskey mash using malt enzymes is:

[a] 140°F – 151°F

[b] 152°F – 160°F

[c] 75°F – 85°F

[d] 173°F – 176°F

8 The mash strike temperature is:

[a] the temperature of the mash during conversion

[b] the temperature of the mash just after the grain is added

[c] the temperature of the mash water before it's heated

[d] the temperature to which the mash water is heated
before the grain is added

9 Sparging is the process of:

[a] agitating the mash during conversion

[b] separating the liquid wort from the grain solids

[c] testing the mash for complete starch conversion

[d] force cooling the mash to fermentation temperature

10 Mashing is:

[a] the biochemical process of converting grain starches to
fermentable sugars

[b] the mechanical process of grinding the grain into a fine powder

[c] the process of blending the different grains of a particular
whiskey recipe

[d] the process of separating the grain from the husk

11 The target Originating Gravity (OG) of a whiskey mash is in the range of:

[a] 1.090 – 1.100

[b] 0.996 – 1.004

[c] 1.060 – 1.070

[d] 1.075 – 1.085

12 The purpose of the yeast in fermentation is to:

[a] impart flavor to the wash

[b] provide nutrients to the fermentation

[c] preserve the mash and prevent spoilage

[d] metabolize the sugars to alcohol and other organic compounds

13 The definition of "mash" is:

[a] the substrate during the mashing and fermentation stages

[b] the grain when it's ready for the mashing process

[c] the spent grain after the mashing process is complete

[d] the substrate when it's ready to go into the still

14 The definition of "wash" is:

[a] the liquid rinsed from the grain after the mashing is complete

[b] the spent liquid in the still boiler after the distillation is finished

[c] the mash after it's fermented and ready to be distilled

[d] the hot water used to sparge the grain

15 Oxygen dissolved in the mash during aeration:

[a] supplies an important molecular building block of alcohol

[b] facilitates the break-down of sugar to alcohol

[c] is necessary for the yeast to reproduce during the aerobic phase of the fermentation

[d] contributes to the flavor profile of the whiskey

16 Distillation is a process whereby:

[a] a fermented substrate is left very still so the sediment can separate out

[b] a chemical reaction takes place that produces a high concentration of alcohol

[c] the alcohol is filtered out of the substrate

[d] the compounds in a substrate are separated based on their different boiling points

17. The type of still most suited to producing whiskey is:

[a] a gooseneck still

[b] a high-separation fractionating still

[c] a continuous-run cracking tower

[d] none of the above

18 The packing in a reflux column serves the purpose of:

[a] cooling the vapors as they rise up the column

[b] providing surfaces for a vapor-liquid interface that effects hundreds of thousands of little mini-distillations

[c] filtering out impurities

[d] to slow the flow of vapor up the column

19 A dephlegmator is a component that:

[a] removes phlegm from the distillate in the column

[b] increases reflux in a distillation column by force cooling the vapors near the top of the column

[c] reacts out sulfides in the alcohol vapor

[d] condenses the vapor back to a liquid as it exits the still

20 Spirits like vodka and gin are unique in that:

[a] they are made from pure ethanol

[b] they are simply whiskey that hasn't been aged in a barrel

[c] their flavor is derived entirely from the feedstock from which they're made

[d] they are fermented at a lower temperature

21 Bubble-cap trays serve the purpose of:

[a] aerating the vapors in the column

[b] adding water to the distillate

[c] condensing the vapors

[d] creating reflux the same as packing does in small columns

22 The shape of a still:

[a] has no effect on the flavor of the finished spirit

[b] is for aesthetic appeal only

[c] plays a significant role in the character of the spirit

[d] is purely a matter of operational preference

23 The shape of the pot affects:

[a] how the wash is heated

[b] the alcohol content of the finished spirit

[c] the boiling point of the wash

[d] the vapor pressure in the column

24 The length and shape of the swan neck of a pot still affects:

[a] the time it takes for the still to come to boil

[b] the boiling point of the wash

[c] the level of separation of the still

[d] none of the above

25 Shorter-necked stills yield spirits that are:

[a] fuller-bodied and creamier

[b] lighter, more fragrant

[c] more neutral in flavor

[d] higher in alcohol

26 The ogee, or boil bowl, at the bottom of the neck of a still serves as:

[a] a trap to catch solids

[b] a chamber for rising vapors to heat up

[c] a chamber for botanicals

[d] an expansion chamber to increase separation

27 Heating a still with more heat:

[a]   increases the throughput but reduces the degree of reflux

[b]   increases the degree of reflux but decreases the throughput

[c]   increases both the throughput and the degree of reflux

[d]   decreases both the throughput and the degree of reflux

28 By extending the lyne arm at an upward incline, this:

[a]   decreases reflux

[b]   increases reflux

[c]   chills the vapors

[d]   has no effect

29 60% of the whiskey's flavor profiles is contributed by:

[a]   barrel aging

[b]   the type of yeast

[c]   barley variety

[d]   shape of the spirit still

30 When distilling whiskey, congeners are present in:

[a]   heads

[b]   hearts

[c]   tails

[d]   all of the above

31. The fusel alcohols, which are known for causing hangovers, come out of the still in their highest concentration in the:

[a]   heads phase

[b]   hearts phase

[c]   tails phase

[d]   beer-stripping run only

32 Acetone and methanol, which is often present, comes out of the still in their highest concentration in the:

[a]   heads phase

[b]   hearts phase

[c]   tails phase

[d]   beer-stripping run only

33 "Feints" are the compounds from a distillation that:

[a]   make one light-headed and pass out

[b]   occur in only tiny, trace amounts

[c]   are the combined heads and tails

[d]   are used in a subsequent sour-mash process

34 At the end of a spirit run to produce whiskey,
     the actual whiskey is the:

[a]   residue left in the boiler

[b]   heads

[c]   hearts

[d]   tails

35 All of the flavor in a whiskey, before it's aged in barrels,
     comes from:

[a]   the congeners

[b]   infusions added to the whiskey after it's distilled

[c]   botanicals placed in the still

[d]   the alcohol

36 "Low-wine" is:

[a]   another name for the fermented mash

[b]   the output from the beer-stripping run

[c]   a wine that's substandard and is distilled to recover its alcohol

[d]   whiskey before it's aged in barrels

37 "Making the cuts" refers to:

[a]   the process of judging when to switch from heads to
       hearts and from hearts to tails

[b]   diluting the whiskey before it goes into barrels

[c]   diluting the whiskey to its bottling strength

[d]   judging which barrels of whiskey make the cut for
       the best products

38 To measure the percent alcohol at the parot means:

[a] to measure the percent alcohol in the receiver

[b] to measure the percent alcohol that is presently flowing from the still

[c] to measure the percent alcohol in the barrel

[d] to measure the percent alcohol of the liquid loaded into the boiler

39 During a whiskey distillation run, the percent alcohol of the distillate:

[a] increases as the distillation progresses

[b] fluctuates at first and then stays constant for the rest of the run

[c] varies with each phase of the distillation

[d] decreases as the distillation progresses

40 During the barrel-aging process, the whiskey can take on a bitterness due to:

[a] lignins

[b] tannin

[c] vanillins

[d] oxidation

41 The optimum percent-alcohol range for aging whiskey in a new barrel is:

[a] 85 – 95%

[b] 40 – 50%

[c] 55 – 65%

[d] 70 – 80%

42 A low-humidity barrel warehouse results in:

[a] an increase in percent alcohol

[b] a decrease in the amount of vanillin extraction, and generally poorer whiskey

[c] an increase in vanillin extraction, and generally better whiskey

[d] a tendency for the barrel to leak

43 A higher-temperature barrel warehouse:

[a] results in a poor-quality whiskey

[b] decreases the rate of oxidation

[c] may result in aging not taking place at all

[d] results in faster aging of the whiskey and
is therefore advantageous

44 Most Scottish malt whiskies are aged in barrels made of:

[a] used American white oak staves

[b] European oak staves

[c] red oak staves

[d] dark oak staves

45 Under US law, bourbon must be aged in:

[a] toasted oak barrels

[b] new charred oak barrels

[c] lightly charred oak barrels

[d] heavily toasted oak barrels

46 The "angels' share" is:

[a] the amount of whiskey lost due to evaporation

[b] the profits lost to excise tax

[c] the special casks reserved for nobility

[d] the whiskey consumed by the distillery workers

47 A standard whiskey barrel in the United States is:

[a] 40 gallons

[b] 53 gallons

[c] 31 gallons

[d] 45 gallons

48 Barrels that are smaller than the standard distillery size:

[a] age the whiskey slower

[b] impart a harsh flavor to the whiskey

[c] age the whiskey faster

[d] make no difference to the aging process

49 A whiskey barrel that's been empty for a while will often:

[a] lose its ability to mature whiskey

[b] require re-charring

[c] impart an undesirable flavor

[d] be dried out and leak between the staves

50 Before barrel aging, whiskey should be diluted to
     the desired strength with:

[a] pure water

[b] feints

[c] tails

[d] low-wine

51 The best locations to barrel-age whiskey are:

[a] hot, dry places that experience temperature swings

[b] cool, humid places that maintain a constant temperature

[c] dark places, shaded from sunlight

[d] moist places that keep the barrels from drying out

52 After the whiskey has been aging for awhile, but is not yet mature,
     the whiskey will:

[a] have a weak watery taste

[b] have a raw woody taste, and will have a burnt flavor

[c] taste like finished whiskey, but will have no color

[d] taste like vodka, but will have a little color

53 When periodically tasting whiskey in the barrels to determine if it's
     mature, the taster:

[a] can judge by color development alone

[b] should taste the whiskey mixed with a drink mixer
       like cola or inger ale

[c] should cleanse their pallet by biting on a slice of lemon first

[d] should nose and taste the whiskey at full strength, and then
       diluted half-and-half with water

54 The impurities that make up the flavor of the whiskey:

[a]   are basically a combination of late heads and early tails congeners

[b]   come only from the tails

[c]   come only from the heads

[d]   are not present at all in the heads and tails.

55 Scottish and Irish style malt whiskies are aged in used barrels because:

[a]   the staves are tighter and there's less chance of leakage

[b]   they are cheaper than new ones

[c]   new barrels would impart an overpowering oak character to the delicate malt flavor

[d]   because used barrels age the whiskey faster

ANSWERS

1. [d]	11. [c]	21. [d]	31. [c]	41. [c]	51. [a]
2. [c]	12. [d]	22. [c]	32. [a]	42. [c]	52. [b]
3. [a]	13. [a]	23. [a]	33. [c]	43. [d]	53. [d]
4. [c]	14. [c]	24. [c]	34. [c]	44. [a]	54. [a]
5. [c]	15. [c]	25. [a]	35. [a]	45. [b]	55. [c]
6. [b]	16. [d]	26. [d]	36. [b]	46. [a]	
7. [a]	17. [a]	27. [a]	37. [a]	47. [b]	
8. [d]	18. [b]	28. [b]	38. [b]	48. [c]	
9. [b]	19. [b]	29. [a]	39. [d]	49. [d]	
10. [a]	20. [a]	30. [d]	40. [b]	50. [a]	

I

Logs

Distilling Logs to Maintain

BOTTLING FILL LOG

Date _____

Product _____

Number of Bottles _____

Number of Cases _____

Fill _____

Alcohol Measure _____

Notes_____

_____
Filling done by

DISTILLING LOG

Volume of Wash _____ % Alcohol _____

Time to Alcohol Boil _____

Temperature of Heads cut. _____ Alc. _____

Run time for the Hearts— Start _____ Stop_____

Hearts Volume _____ Alc. _____

Temperature at Tails Cut _____

Total Time, Start to Finish _____

_____
(signed) Distiller

WASH LOG BOOK

Date: _____

Distilling Wash: 40 gallons

Grains: 125 lbs.

80% 2-row barley

10% flaked barley

5% 2-row Munich.

Strike Water: 40 gallons @ 170 degrees

Mash-in Temperature: 157 degrees

Sparge Water Temp: 170 degrees

Original Gravity: 1.068

Yeast Type: Ale yeast from White Labs

Fermentation: 72 Degrees

Days of Fermentation: 7 days

Final Gravity: 1.006

Wash Alcohol: 8.1%

Notes (or) wash evaluation

_____

_____

_____

GAUGING LOG

to 60 proof	0.07463
to 120 proof	0.15776
to 70 proof	0.08764
to 82 proof	0.10362
to 83 proof	0.10498

Batch:

Date:

Stripping
Rec
Rec/Gin

Gauging Log

Bulk - Tables 1-2-3-7

Date	Hyd. Reading	Temp	Adj. Proof Table 1	WT	Tare	Adj. WT	PG Table 2 or 3	Adj. Factor Table 7	Adj. PG	Notes
						#VALUE!			####	
						0				
						0				
						0				
						0				

Reduction Tables 2-4

Date	Spirit Weight From Above	PG From Above	New Target Proof	PG per LB Table 4	PG/PG per LB	Lb of H2O	Total Tank Weight	Notes
	#VALUE!				#VALUE!	#VALUE!		
	0	0			#DIV/0!	#DIV/0!		
	0	0			#DIV/0!	#DIV/0!		
	0	0			#DIV/0!	#DIV/0!		

Final Guage in Package

Cases:
Extra Bottles:

Notes:

J

Floor Plan

FLOOR PLAN
CRAFT WHISKEY DISTILLERY
8,000 Sq. Ft./10,000 Cases

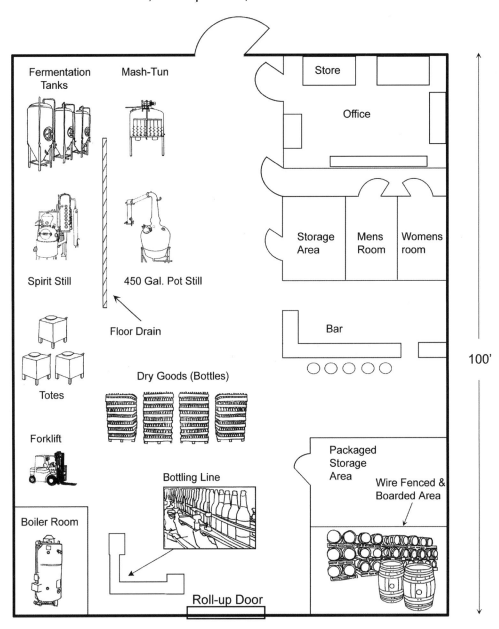

Photographs

CPSIA information can be obtained
at www.ICGtesting.com
Printed in the USA
LVIW02n2103280813
350084LV00003B

9 780982 405512